WHERE THE HEART IS

Stories of Home and Family

Chick Moorman

PERSONAL
POWER
PRESS

Personal Power Press
Saginaw, Michigan

WHERE THE HEART IS
Stories of Home and Family

© 1996 by Chick Moorman and Personal Power Press

Library of Congress Catalogue
Card Number   ISBN
95-70904   0-9616046-3-8

PERSONAL
POWER
PRESS

Printed in the United States of America
Personal Power Press
P.O. Box 5985
Saginaw, MI 48603

Cover Design by Elizabeth J. Nagel

I would like to thank and acknowledge the following publishers for permission to use the following material.

"Accumulated Dividends" and "I Said It Couldn't Be Done." Used by permission of Rosita Perez. Reprinted from *The Music Is You: A Guide to Thinking Less and Feeling More* by Rosita Perez. Published by Trudy Knox, Granville, OH. © 1981 Rosita Perez.

"All the Comforts of Nome," "Logophilia," "Mother's Tabernacle Choir," and "The Wizards of Nations Creek." Reprinted by permission of Ben Burton. Excerpted from *The Chicken That Won a Dogfight* by Ben Burton. Published by August House Publishers, Inc., Little Rock. © 1993 Ben Burton.

"Choosing Who We Are" and "The Family That Laughs Together." Reprinted by permission of Naomi Rhode. Reprinted from *The Gift of Family: A Legacy of Love* by Naomi Rhode. Published by Thomas Nelson Publishers, Nashville. © 1991 Naomi Rhode.

"Collecting Memories." Reprinted by permission of Leo Buscaglia. Excerpted from *Born for Love* by Leo F. Buscaglia, Ph.D. Published by Slack, Inc. © 1992 Leo F. Buscaglia, Inc. and *Living, Loving, and Learning* by Leo F. Buscaglia, Ph.D. Published by Slack, Inc. © 1982 Leo F. Buscaglia, Inc.

"Jerry, Jr." Reprinted by permission of Gerald Coffee. Excerpted from *Beyond Survival* by Gerald Coffee. Published by Coffee Enterprises. © 1990 Gerald Coffee.

"The Signal." Reprinted by permission of Stan Dale. Excerpted from *My Child, My Self: How to Raise the Child You Always Wanted to Be* by Stan Dale. Published by Human Awareness Publications, San Mateo, CA 94402. © 1992 Human Awareness Publications.

"This is Better Than Meditation." Reprinted by permission of Terry Wooten. Reprinted from *The Stone Circle Anthology—Poems for Big Blue*, Published by Stone Circle Press, © 1995.

DEDICATION

To my daughter, Jenny, with love, appreciation, and admiration. Thank you for providing my dad—your grandfather—with a continuous atmosphere of love and caring during his final year of life. You gave him dignity, purpose, family, and a meaningful place in his own home. When it comes to home and family, I am the student, and you are my teacher.

FOREWORD

Families come in many sizes, shapes, and colors, and parenting comes in many forms—traditional, single, step-, and foster, among others. As a father of three boys, I can attest to the fact that none of it is easy. Unfortunately, children don't come with an owner's manual that makes a family work smoothly and efficiently at all times. In addition, few parents get any skill-training in raising compassionate and responsible children.

Families have received a lot of bad press in recent years; "dysfunctional" is a word often used to describe them. The divorce rate is too high. Child abuse is prevalent. This book, *Where the Heart Is*, has a different message. It shares the good news about families. It celebrates commitment, connectedness, integrity, and love at a time when the world most needs to hear about these important values.

Chicken Soup for the Soul, which I wrote with Mark Victor Hansen, became a *New York Times* bestseller in part because the world is ready for good news, warmth, and inspiration. *Where the Heart Is,* the book you now hold in your hands, provides just that. It helps us learn how to build healthy family relationships by reading about other healthy families. It inspires as well as gives practical examples for building a positive family life.

My longtime friend and colleague, Chick Moorman, has compiled a moving collection of uplifting vignettes and usable ideas that you can put to work immediately in your family. The gift he has given us is the possibility of more intimacy, love, and connectedness among family members around the world.

I am thrilled you are reading this book. I promise you it will make a positive difference in your life.

Jack Canfield
Co-Author, *Chicken Soup for the Soul*

PREFACE

This book is about the importance of family.

- It celebrates family strength, love, tolerance, hope, and commitment.

- It focuses on what is good and noble about parenting. It reveals a model of parenting that nurtures, uplifts, and inspires, producing respect among all family members.

- It communicates the warmth and dignity inherent in positive family relationships.

It is a book that features families that work.

Where the Heart Is: Stories of Home and Family consists of vignettes, articles, poems, and cartoons contributed by generous, caring people filled with a desire to share how or why their family matters. Some stories are serious. Others are humorous. All are intended to instruct, inform, and reinforce the notion that family does, indeed, matter.

As you read the book, notice the thoughts and feelings that each story elicits. How does the story affect you? Where does it touch you? What memories, ideas, goals, and gut level reactions does it prompt? Attempt to connect personally with the writer.

Allow these stories to move you to action. If you feel like calling your mother, do it. If you get the urge to apologize to your son, do it. If you feel compelled to write to one of the contributors, go for it. You will find their biographical information and addresses at the end of the book. If you are overwhelmed by the desire to buy copies of *Where the Heart Is* for all your friends and relatives, let nothing get in your way.

I began work on this book three years ago. I was living with my wife, two stepchildren, and my youngest son. When problems developed in my marriage, I stopped writing. I also stopped doing parenting workshops. I felt hypocritical and phony. I could not face a room full of parents and tell them how to do what I was unable to do in my own life with my own family. Also, many of the examples I used in my speaking were personal, and the emotions they brought up at that time were more than I wanted to deal with in front of a room full of people.

When my marriage failed, I joined a men's group, got regular counseling, and began line dancing. (Line dancing is great therapy. Lots of kicking, stomping, scuffing, and heel grinding.) I rebuilt my support group, reconnected with myself and others, and began to come back.

In the middle of the recovery process, my mother was diagnosed with liver cancer. She lived for six weeks. Watching my dad watch my mom die had a major impact on me. The gentle love and concern he showed was a model I'll never forget.

My mother's death had a unifying effect on the entire family. It brought us together with love and caring in a way no other single event ever did.

The loss of my primary family unit and my mother, coupled with reconnecting to my family of origin, helped me regain my focus on the importance of family. I resumed my parenting workshops and found that my speaking had a new spirit and sense of direction. I took my unfinished manuscript off the shelf and recommitted myself to the effort of completing it. I set a goal of creating a national bestseller that would help strengthen families worldwide.

As I went back to work, I felt somewhat like a wounded horse summoned to battle in the king's service. Still healing, I yet heeded the call and began limping toward my goal. The farther along the path I travelled, the stronger I became.

Soon gifts began appearing along the way in the form of insights and contributions. I put out a request for stories, and miracles started appearing in my mailbox daily. Many of them are included in this book. Several people attached messages which said, in essence: *I don't even care if you publish this. Just writing it has been worth it for me. Thank you for the opportunity.* When I needed to learn about marketing, the opportunity appeared. When I needed money, it showed up. When I needed encouragement, that was there, too.

Even before I realized I needed an editor, she appeared. Nancy Lewis learned of the project when her husband, a speaker, received my letter soliciting stories. Nancy is a writer and editor. She read the sample story I had enclosed with the solicitation and wrote me applauding my idea and concept. She also wrote, "The story about your grandfather has a lot of potential but loses its power through awkward phrasing, grammatical weaknesses, and inappropriate word choices. I've taken the liberty of editing it and giving it a stronger title so you can judge for yourself whether you feel my observation has merit." I liked what she had done and called her. We joined forces, and what a gift she has been. Her editing skill, advice, and encouragement have been an ongoing miracle. It was Nancy who suggested the book's title.

I began compiling *Where the Heart Is* for you and your family. Somewhere along the way I realized that I was involved in this process for me and my family. It has been an incredible act of healing for me. It has helped me figure out who I am and what I want to be as a man, a parent, and a grandfather. It has provided me with vision and purpose. It has helped me grow closer to God and the spiritual principles that are so important to love and family.

During the creation of this book I have reached out to my father, and he has responded with a new level of intimacy. I know now why so many grown men sent me stories about their fathers. I have connected with my grown children in new and deeply satisfying ways. Miracles continue to occur in my family life, and my own heart has been greatly affected.

Family and home can and should be where the heart is. May reading and sharing this book help your own heart come home.

Chick Moorman

ACKNOWLEDGEMENTS

This book was not a one-person effort. It took the energy of many people to create. My sincere thanks go to the following: Debbie Dukarski, my office manager and friend whose encouragement and belief sustained me during personal and professional crises. It was Debbie who took this book concept off the shelf when I had abandoned it, put it back in my hands, and convinced me it was needed in the world.

Peggy Lange learned to decipher most of my illegible handwriting and typed and retyped mountains of copy. Her proofreading and computer wizardry have helped immensely in bringing the book you hold in your hands to print.

Several people gave valuable feedback on the stories, reading and rating them so those with the most universal appeal would be included. My thanks to Mike Assels, Sue Dabakey, Kathleen Dukarski, Val Haller, Carol Inman, Beth Jerry, Kathy Jordan, Sara Knapp, Linda Moorman, Tom Moorman, Ann Newmann, and Susan Omdahl.

I extend my warmest gratitude to the over 300 people who responded to my call for stories and vignettes. I am deeply touched by the tremendous outpouring of sharing and caring my request prompted. The entries you see here represent only a portion of the stories I received. Sadly, space, format, and theme precluded my using all the submissions; consequently, many warm and uplifting stories had to be left out. I appreciate each contributor's willingness to share such intimate and moving experiences with me and with all of you. Thank you all.

Nancy Lewis, whose editing talent put the frosting on many of the stories you'll read here, is the real star of this book. Her background as an English teacher, writer, and editor, along with her personal mission of helping people preserve their life stories, added a much-needed touch to *Where the Heart Is*. I recommend that you read Nancy's bio in the contributors' section and use her skills for your own writing projects. Her expertise and commitment were highly appreciated.

CONTENTS

I. TIES THAT BIND

III. MOTHERS, continued

IV. GRANDPARENTS

V. LESSONS

V. LESSONS, continued

VI. HEROES

I.

TIES

THAT

BIND

AMAZING GRACE

Fran O'Connell

Rebecca was almost three when she came to live with us. Her mother—my husband's sister —had been killed in a car accident. She had not married Rebecca's father, and Rebecca had a limited relationship with him.

She was a tiny thing, with enormous brown eyes and long, thick lashes that belonged in a Maybelline commercial. She spoke very little, and what little she did say was often profane. She had few social skills, even for a three-year-old. She hit and bit and punched and kicked—eyebrows furrowed and black anger glowing from those beautiful eyes. Except for the use of the "f-word," which—amazingly—was always contextually correct, she seemed unable to express herself. She never cried. She took in all that happened quietly. She watched. And she waited.

Rebecca's brother and sister also moved in with us. While all three children had behavior problems, it was Rebecca who seemed most clearly to have experienced abuse and neglect.

After examining her, our pediatrician pronounced her "developmentally delayed." I told him I thought it was more than that; the child was clearly language-impaired but otherwise seemed exceptionally bright. The doctor disagreed. Speaking gently and kindly, smiling at Rebecca as he talked, he said she was "slow." Rebecca gave him the finger. This child was not slow! After further psychological exams and therapy, it became clear that Rebecca had been abused, but she was too young to sort out her experience. In response, she had developed a generalized fear of adults. She didn't want to sit on my lap. She screamed when my husband came into the room. She fought with the other kids all the time.

About the only time she seemed to feel safe was when I put her to bed each night. She had a ritual: PJs, brush teeth, wash hands, turn out the light, sing two songs. Her favorites were "Danny Boy" and "Amazing Grace." Night after night, month after month, year after year, we sang the songs. In a way, the struggles, the sorrow, the triumph of the songs paralleled my own experiences as I came to terms with the changes in my life and the lives of my children.

School, at first, presented more problems. Rebecca almost got expelled from kindergarten for her behavior. She spent most of first grade in the office with the school secretary. But then things started to improve. Not only was she learning to read and to reason, she was learning how to trust and to love.

When she started second grade, we switched schools. By this time, Rebecca was doing well, academically and socially. She even joined the

Brownies and took pride in belonging to a social group for the very first time. We kept singing.

In April of her second grade year, Rebecca made her First Communion. The communicants and their families were the first to receive the sacrament. Looking beautiful in her white dress, with a wreath of flowers in her curly brown hair, Rebecca took my hand. As we walked to the altar, the organist began playing "Amazing Grace."

Rebecca looked up at me. "They're playing our song, Ma," she said brightly. "It's my favorite song in the whole world, and they're playing it just for us!"

In that instant, I remembered the endless nights. The nights I was too tired to sing and I told Rebecca to sing for us both. The nights I prayed, "Just let me get through the songs, Lord." The nights I cried with her, for her, about her. The nights we sang together, "'Twas grace that kept us safe thus far, and grace will lead us home."

It took four years to see trust in those beautiful, dark eyes. Four years of amazing grace.♥

COLLECTING MEMORIES

Leo Buscaglia

Our family was a very strange one because sometimes we were flying high, and we had *everything* we wanted—ravioli, and gnocchi, and spaghetti, and sausages, everything we wanted—and other times there was practically nothing. We'd make a great polenta. You know polenta? It's a northern Italian dish that's a big cake made of corn meal, and it's very filling. Six bites and you're dragging! But at least your stomach doesn't hurt!

But we were never protected against pain, because every time Papa walked in, and we'd see on my father's face a long, long, long expression, he'd say something like "We don't have any more money." Then he would add, "What are *we* going to do about it?" Oh, it was so nice to see everybody get together as a "we." My sister would say, "I'll go to the market and collect the leftover leaves for the rabbits." And I became a vendor of magazines. Remember when we used to sell magazines from door to door? Boy, what an education that was. And everybody did something. We experienced the togetherness.

Mama used to do a wonderful thing. She knew how to deal with Papa's long faces. She had a little thing she called a survival bottle. She used to put a little bit of money in a bottle and bury it in the backyard for the day when we were starving. Then she used to do something *outrageous* with that money! All of a sudden she'd bring in a chicken!

But we learned a lot from despair. We learned a lot from hunger. We learned a lot by being taken in as a "we" and made a part of a family.

****

Mama used to encourage us to collect as many memories of happiness as we could. She assured us that they would come in handy during the times when things were not going so well. And she practiced what she preached. When hard times struck, she would remind us that there were happier days ahead. She also had a wonderful talent of turning painful experiences into positive ones.

One occasion comes instantly to mind. Papa informed us one evening that his business partner had absconded with their funds, leaving him bankrupt and deeply in debt. Of course, our whole family was distressed by this news. How would we pay our bills? Where would we get our next meal?

The following evening Mama answered that last question. She prepared the most elaborate feast we had seen in months. Papa was furious. "Have you gone crazy?" he angrily demanded.

"No," Mama replied, "I just thought it was a perfect time for celebration. This is when we need to be happy the most! We'll survive."

And survive we did. In addition to a practical lesson, Mama also gave us all a beautiful memory which has served us well over these many years. No one in our family will ever forget that dinner.♥

A TOGETHER FAMILY

Amy Kavanaugh
Age 14

My mom's boyfriend is always saying, "All I want is a normal life, with a normal girlfriend and her normal family." And then my mom says, "Then you obviously have the wrong girlfriend and her family."

That is so true. Things are always happening to my family. Like on St. Patrick's Day this year a friend of mine got hit in the head with a rock and had to get stitches.

My family is there for me when I need them, and I'm there for them. We're a together family and know where we are when we need each other.

I'm glad that I have the family I do instead of a boring family that nothing happens in.♥

ALL THE COMFORTS OF NOME

Ben Burton

Last winter let me down hard. It was one of the mildest ever recorded and I sure was disappointed. I was all primed and hoping for a real winter, the kind we had when I was growing up.

How long has it been since you've had a coating of snow dust down through the shingles at night and your hair stiffened as you slept? How many of you have sung and laughed with your brother or sister through chattering teeth? My brother, Len, and I chattered a great "Stars and Stripes Forever." Len was better than some on that runaway piccolo part.

Or how long has it been since you've had one of your parents tuck a warm brick under the covers up next to your cold feet? I never felt more loved than then. Parents don't have that opportunity much any more, and it's hard to replace it when it comes to expressing love.

My theory and firm belief is that it's good for us all to be really cold once in awhile in our life.

Gives us something to lean against and something to look forward to—back on, as well. That old house we lived in when we were growing up provided those advantages. So much cold and so many warm memories.

My wife and I recently built a new home and paid a lot of extra money to have a wood-burning fireplace put in it. You know that's what people do now days even in the best houses. Why we had a wood-burning fireplace in that old house we lived in years ago. We were way ahead of our time. Of course we didn't have central heat to keep the fireplace warm. I wasn't warm on both sides at once until I went to college.

Quilts were necessities, not just conversational items. A winter night was measured by the number of quilts it took to survive it. "A four-quilt night back in '98" was a favorite embellishment for one of the great tales my Daddy told. A three-quilter was the worst winter night I remember. That night is memorable, not for the cold, but for the two or three warm brick exchanges that occurred just at the right time.

My wife recently bought a patchwork quilt. It's nice, but it's only decorative. I doubt we will ever have to use it to keep warm.

I started this piece out by saying that I regret we didn't have a harder winter. It got me to thinking about that old house we grew up in. If it hadn't finally fallen down, our old house may have, by now, been on the National Register of Historic Places. That old house may have been the place about which someone wrote, "It's not a house that makes a home."

No, a house doesn't make a home, but I know several things that do. One of them is the reason I was yearning for an extra cold winter last year. I was all set for it with our new fireplace, a lot of wood—and a plan.

My plan was to wait until it got really cold one night, new fireplace and all. After everyone turned in, I was going to flip the central heat off and help the house get as cold as our old house used to get. Maybe I would even open a window or two to let some of the winter get inside like it did back then.

I was going to get up in that cold house and warm an old brick I've kept for this purpose. When the brick got just right, I was going to wrap it in a piece of flannel cloth and ease it under the covers and up to my granddaughter's tiny feet.

Even after she has lived as long as I have, she will never feel any more loved than she will at that moment. And that warm memory will bond her forever to me and to our house. That will be good for her—and great for me.

Maybe next year.♥

JERRY, JR.

Gerald Coffee

In the late summer of 1967 I had been moved from the old French-built headquarters prison, Hoa Lo, in downtown Hanoi to one of the several smaller makeshift prisons in the suburbs of the city. We called this one the "Zoo." The following excerpt from my book, *Beyond Survival*, took place during the fall of 1967.

April 2nd, 1967

Dear Jerry,

The weather here for early spring has been beautiful. The flowers have been blooming already and we're looking forward to Easter.

We miss you all the more when we're at the lake, sometimes with friends and sometimes just as a family. The kids are all doing great. Kim skis all the way around the lake now. The boys swim and dive off

*the dock and little Jerry splashes around
with a little bubble on his back . . .*

Little Jerry!

I stopped reading because my eyes were filling
with tears. I clutched the handwritten letter to my
chest and looked up toward the tiny air vent that
barely allowed sufficient light to read the words
from Bea.

Little Jerry! Who's little Jerry? My voice
cracked as I realized, of course, who Jerry was—
my third son. Yes, if his name is Jerry he must be
a boy, and if he can splash around in the water on
his own he must be healthy. He must have been
born okay. Everything must have gone all right
for Bea. God, I couldn't believe I actually had a
letter from her. She had no way to know that I
had never received any of her previous letters so
this one was written very matter-of-factly, but to
me it was like poetry.

I reread the text several times, my mind
jammed with visions of the reality of her words.
She said all of our family was fine. She and the
kids probably would go to California for the
summer again. The kids are all sweet and happy
and helpful and doing fine in school. And "Jerry
is such a sweet, cute, special little guy. Everyone
just loves him so much. The other kids are so
cute with him."

Oh, God, thank you for my new son.

I thought about his name. We had never
talked about naming a son after me, but I guess
under the circumstances Bea felt it was
appropriate. I thought of the poor little guy

having to go through his life as a Gerald Leonard Coffee, Jr., just because his old man was on ice somewhere in a strange land when he was born. "Gerald Leonard Coffee, Jr.," I repeated, shaking my head slowly and smiling and licking the tears from my lips. I was so pleased. And I was so relieved and gratified to finally know the outcome of Bea's pregnancy, that all had apparently gone well with both her and the baby. Finally my prayers were answered.

The letter concluded:

> *All of us, plus so many others, are praying for your safety and return soon. But we're all fine, so don't worry about us. Our family and friends have been so helpful and loving.*
>
> *You take good care of yourself, Honey. I miss you and love you.*
>
> *Bea*

I sat there in the gloom so full of emotions: relief and thanksgiving for finally knowing; sorrow for missing out on Jerry's entire first year; joy for being the father of—in my context at least —a new baby boy; but mostly gratitude for the blessing of my family—my beautiful children and my wife in whom I had so much confidence and faith. And gratitude for the blessing of simply being alive at this point and for the hope of being reunited with them all again soon. I thought of them and prayed for several hours.

From the beginning, my daily routine had included prayers and actually saying a daily Mass.

As I went through the Mass I always visualized it being celebrated by our priest at Lake Mary Parish back in Florida. Each day I visualized arriving at the church, greeting friends, sitting in the same pew, the kids separated in varying ways by Bea and me. I would visualize the various parts of the Mass and recite the parts I could recall: "*In nomine Patris et Filii et Spiritus Sancti . . . mea culpa, mea culpa, mea maxima culpa . . . Kyrie eleison . . .*" When possible, I would save a bit of rice or bread to take as communion during my Mass. The beauty was that now I could visualize the scene with Jerry included, holding him on my knee when he got a little restless, patting Kimmie on the knee near the lacy hem of her church dress, pressing Steve's cowlick down into place, or winking at Dave's happy face as he pretended to read the hymnal and glanced my way for approval. The picture of my family was now complete. Now I could visualize them all in the present and plan for our future accurately. My plans would provide one of the most bountiful sources of hope and strength in the years to come.

I had by now decided the only thing predictable about the communists was their unpredictability. I had resigned myself to never receiving any of the letters I knew Bea was writing, so this letter had caught me totally by surprise. Happy, our daily turnkey here in the Pool Hall, had simply stepped into my cell very unceremoniously, waited for my bow, handed me the letter, and left. He could have required another bow as he left, but he had undoubtedly noticed my look of disbelief as I stared at the envelope, recognizing Bea's handwriting. He probably realized I was instantly twelve thousand miles from the tiny cell we were both standing in.

A few days after he had delivered the letter, I had been the last to set out my dishes and ended up washing them for the whole cell block. As I reentered my cell, Happy dispensed with the bow, pointed at me, then pointed over my shoulder toward the East and said, "*My,*" the Vietnamese word for America, then defined with both hands the curve of a woman's body. Does Coffee have a woman? I smiled and nodded in the affirmative, duplicating his sign for a woman's body but perhaps accentuating the curves a little more. Then he did the stairstep routine with his hand: Kids? Again I nodded, held up four fingers and did the stairstep from the bottom up, pausing to tell him their ages—*mot, bon, sau, thom;* one, four, six, and eight.

He acknowledged the information with a trace of a smile. "You?" I pointed to him and traced the shape of a woman with my hands. This time he smiled, stepped back so he could glance out the door in both directions to make sure no one was approaching, then fished out his wallet and produced a picture of his girl under clear plastic.

She was pretty but could have been any one of the hundreds I'd seen in the street that first morning en route to Hoa Lo Prison. I oohed and aahed and smiled and pointed to my wedding-ring finger, then to him and her, and looked at him questioningly. "Married?" He shook his head with a look of disgust, swept his arm around over his head, generally indicating the whole damn war situation as the reason they weren't married.

Over the years I would have similar conversations with other guards who were eager to exchange such personal information. But they did so with considerable circumspection. To be caught by a superior would likely lead to immediate reassignment to the front. And by comparison, prison guard duty in Hanoi was a very good deal.

After receiving the letter from Bea, I frequently recalled the night I had returned to the Zoo from Hoa Lo after a few days of interrogation there following the Hanoi March. The warm night air seemed to have been infused with the yellow light of the full moon directly overhead. It illuminated the several low buildings of the Zoo with a soft glow that belied the misery and despair within them. The silvery silhouettes of trees softened the lines of all the structures, and I could even distinguish the colors—lavender and peach—of their various blossoms. Their fragrance sweetened the air.

As if this wasn't startling enough, the cool fragrant air carried—of all things—the breathy voice of Julie London singing "Love Letters." The evening English-language broadcast of the Voice of Vietnam was coming through the speakers in each cell and out through the air vents and louvers, so that it seemed to be coming from no specific source but from everywhere:

Love letters straight from your heart
Keep us so near though apart;
I'm not alone in the night
When I can have all the love you write.

I memorize every line
Then kiss the name that you sign.
Then, darling, once again I read right from the
    start
Love letters straight from your heart.

I read and reread my letter from Bea several times a day. Next to my prayers for her and the children's happiness and well-being, the last thing I would do each night before going to sleep would be to reread her letter. Under the semidarkness of my mosquito net I couldn't really see the words, but I soon had them memorized. I would trace my finger lightly across the lines she had actually penned and I would feel closer to her. And finally, I would kiss the name she had signed.

My family, my memories of them, my thoughts of them, my hopes for them and our future together became the primary driving force for my survival; actually to go beyond survival, to survive and return home to them . . . with honor. It's a good thing, too, because when I received that letter I had no way to know I had over *five years* yet to go; for a total of seven years and nine days.♥

TO BE CONTINUED

Sandra Darling

Sundays! That was my favorite day growing up. I'd wake up early, lured downstairs by the aroma of sizzling bacon and fried sausage. Bread would be popping from the toaster, awaiting a slather of butter. The gurgle of fresh orange juice being poured into tall glasses would greet me. My aunt said our breakfast was always cooked with the best ingredient—love. She was right. I have yet to taste any other home cooking as good.

As the rest of us pitched in to help with the Sunday breakfast routine, my uncle would disappear from the kitchen. After what seemed like forever, we would hear his footsteps on the porch and run to meet him as he reappeared with the Sunday newspaper hugged tightly under his arm. On the outside were the comics, those colorful frames that decorated the rest of the otherwise dull, black-and-white pages. From my viewpoint as a kid, why anyone would notice any other part of the newspaper was beyond me.

We would race through breakfast, pick up and help with the dishes—the sooner the better so we could settle into our Sunday reading time. My uncle would carry the thick, half-folded pile of papers into the living room and we would all surround him. On the couch he'd separate the parts of the paper into piles, according to his interest. The best pile—the comics—landed on his lap.

The four of us would dive for a place on the couch. The best spot was next to my uncle. He made sure we all got our turn. I liked how warm it felt as we all sunk into the couch, cuddled shoulder to shoulder.

As we snuggled, he would begin to read. He read each frame with his own unique sound effects. The comics came alive. I heard the voices of Beetle Bailey, Archie, Dagwood, Little Lulu, Captain America, Nancy and Sluggo.

The comics had become pals gathered around our couch, with a new adventure each Sunday. We clung to each spoken word and anxiously looked ahead to the next frame. We would laugh out loud at the silly situations; I could hear my uncle's laugh above ours. We would follow with our eyes the encapsulated words laced inside a drawn space that looked like a piece of blown bubble gum with a line leading to the comic character who "spoke" them.

At the end of some of the strips, there would be a block of white with the words "To be continued." Those were the adventure stories that we had the most questions about, but my uncle would say, "Wait till next Sunday and you'll see. Now go outside and play!" We would leave with smiles and hopes that the week would go by quickly so we could enjoy another Sunday with my uncle and the comics.♥

THE FAMILY THAT LAUGHS TOGETHER

Naomi Rhode

Our family never tolerated profanity. Jim and I set the example, and the children didn't deviate from the rule.

Except once.

On one of our family trips it seemed like an eternity before we arrived at our destination, Hoover Dam. The temperature was well into the 100s, and nothing we did could cool the car. One unfortunate incident after another seemed to delay our arrival. Finally, after six hours in the car, we pulled into the visitors' parking lot.

"Boy, am I ever glad to be in this dam parking lot," Jim sighed.

Total silence prevailed; we looked at one another with our mouths open.

Then hysteria set in. The kids thought they had caught their dad swearing. Everyone laughed and laughed and laughed and laughed.

"But I meant the *Hoover Dam* parking lot," Jim vainly tried to explain. "It's okay to say 'dam' if you're talking about a particular dam like Hoover Dam."

Inadvertently, Jim had given them permission to say "dam" that day. Never have any visitors laughed so much as our family did as we toured the dam.

"Boy, this *dam* elevator sure is nice," Mark reported. We all laughed.

"Yes, and this *dam* color is very unusual," chimed in Beth. We laughed some more.

"I wonder how many cars this *dam* parking lot holds?" Katherine asked. More gales of laughter followed.

During the whole tour the kids found an incredible number of things to comment on with the word *dam* . . . meaning Hoover, of course.

Silly? Yes. Funny? Yes. Maybe not to you, but to our family it was hysterical because their father had "violated" one of our household's sacred rules and they could follow his example and take advantage of his apparent slip-up.

It's a private joke, but one which never fails to bring laughter to all of us, even 15 years later, anytime we think about it or mention it. Families need private jokes. Things to laugh about that no one else understands or appreciates. Private jokes and shared laughter are one of the bonds that holds a family together.♥

THE 25-CENT CONNECTION

Peggy L. Rolfsmeyer

When our sons were old enough to begin going out by themselves, we had a rule that said they didn't leave the house without a quarter. This quarter was to be used to call us anytime they were in a situation where they felt unsafe or uncomfortable. Our promise to them was that we would pick them up anytime, anywhere, with no questions asked for 24 hours unless they initiated the discussion.

One night we did receive a call. Our oldest son was at a sleep-over where alcohol was beginning to be part of the "fun." Although he didn't need to use a pay phone for the call, he said, "I'm using my quarter and want to come home."

Both boys are now living away from home, in two different states. In their wallets, each still carries a quarter.♥

THE IMPORTANCE OF FAMILY HISTORY

Jim Lamancusa
Age 15

Family history is like a snowflake; no two are the same. To me, knowing your family history gives you a sense of belonging. You need to have memories of your own, as well as the memories given to you by your parents and grandparents. Our family recently made a video of my brother and me asking our grandparents questions about their lives as children and adults: Where did they go to school? Did they have homework? What kinds of jobs did they have to do around the house? What did they do to "just hang out" with their friends?

We shared our similarities and differences about what it was like to be a teenager. They used to play stickball. I run track. I learned that my grandfather was in a Nazi work camp when he was just a little older than I am. He had to escape.

It was interesting to find that I still have some relatives in Europe. I wonder if I'll ever get to meet them. I wonder what they'll be like if I do.

Every family should work on building its own history, then recording it so all the kids that follow will know their roots. It made me feel more secure knowing that there is a long past that helped shape me into who I am today. I'm going to try to continue this process in the future.♥

THANK GOD FOR LIGHTBULBS

John M. Schmitt

Bedtime is one of my favorite parts of the day. It's when my three daughters and I share some special time together. Even though many nights I feel totally exhausted, I do my best to summon the energy to be enthusiastic as we undergo our nightly ritual. After reading a book or two, we share what happened during the day just finished and our plans for the next. Then it's time for family prayers. We always begin by thanking God for the day behind us. Then we take turns asking Him to help people we know who are having problems, or we give special thanks for people or things for which we are most grateful.

Every night we can count on Kellie (age three-and-a-half) to thank God for lightbulbs! For the longest time we couldn't figure out the reason, and we never thought to ask her. A psychologist friend suggested that Kellie might be afraid of the dark, a common fear at her age. We asked Kellie about it the very next night and, sure enough, she confirmed the psychologist's suspicion.

We've stopped chuckling over her lightbulb prayer, and we're even leaving the hall light on a little longer.

Kellie won't always be afraid of the dark, but long after she's stopped thanking God for lightbulbs, I'll continue to give thanks for the lightbulbs of my life: Susann, Kellie, Jenna, and their mom.

Thank God for lightbulbs!♥

THE ANGEL ON TOP OF THE CHRISTMAS TREE

Kathy Lamancusa

It's hard to believe how a simple object made with a cardboard frame, paper silhouette, angel hair, and foil can be so important in the life of a family; how family history can be made and taught through a little angel who sits on top of a tree and watches the world change from year to year.

When I was a very young girl I sat and watched the angel in its place on top of my grandparents' Christmas tree. The memory is forever entwined with the smell of holiday baking and the taste of the wonderful ethnic foods made from recipes my grandmother brought from "the old country."

My grandparents died before my children had a chance to know them. All I asked for of their possessions was the Christmas tree angel. She is how my boys have come to know their great-grandparents.

Each Christmas we all sit together, snuggled on the couch, and we talk as we watch the lights of the tree in the darkened room. The boys ask about the grandma and grandpa who owned the angel, and I tell them the stories. Stories of coming across the ocean on a boat and living in a country in which they didn't even know the language. Stories of courage and hope—of building a family here while never again seeing the family they left behind.

Over 40 years, the angel has needed occasional "cosmetic surgery" to keep her intact. Her glue dries out, and her cardboard frame tends to sag. Repairs are made, and once again she sits on top of the tree, just as she did every year of my childhood.

My son has already asked to have the angel someday. He wants to place it on top of his family's tree each year. He says he'll sit with his children and tell them all about us and his grandparents and his great-grandparents. He says he'll repair the angel whenever she needs it. And someday she'll be passed on to one of his children, and family history will continue to be made and taught.♥

A DIFFERENT KIND OF CHRISTMAS

Sidney B. Simon

I have a strong aversion to Christmases where kids dive under the tree, jerking their loot out, greedily tearing open packages and scattering the mess everywhere. Worse than that, by 10 a.m. they're bored. It's the way to raise what-did-you-buy-me/get-me/give-me children.

So what's the alternative? There's at least one, and when our kids were little, we tried it.

We changed the focus from the receiver to the giver. Each kid would have a time set aside when he or she gave their gifts to each member of the family. They could take as long as they wanted to, talking about how they chose what they were giving and why it was to be precious to the receiver.

After one kid gave, we'd take time out for breakfast. Then another kid would get to be the "giver." Then we'd often go for a walk, and when we came back one of the kids might play the role of "giver" for an absent aunt or other relative.

They'd "play" the aunt, mimicking her accent or her moralizing way of talking, and they'd explain why she sent what she sent. Sometimes it was hilarious—even downright disrespectful—but it was always playful and fun.

And so the day went, with long stretches in between the gift-giving. Maybe we'd look at old 8 mm movies. Everyone looked forward to that. And slides. I suspect every family has one person who enjoys slides more than the rest of the family. In our family, it was me. I'd always say, "Just one more box," and everybody else would groan. But they would miss them if we didn't do them.

Finally, well after dinner, Mom and Dad would get the chance to give the presents we'd accumulated for the brood. We both tried to make with our own hands at least one gift for each kid. That, in itself, was worth celebrating.

Christmas at our house, when the kids were little, was long and sweet. I hope they remember it the way I do: filled with family and filled with the spirit of giving rather than with the acquisition of loot. Isn't that the way it should be?♥

TRASH CAN KIDS

Rick Benedict

As an educator, I am concerned about the high school dropout problem and about students who, for whatever reason, have decided traditional schooling is not for them. Several years ago I designed a program I thought might meet the needs of those students. I started an alternative high school aimed at getting young people off the streets and back into school. This project focused not on students currently having trouble in school but rather on those who had already dropped out—or been dropped. The school staff literally went out into the streets and talked dropouts into giving school one final opportunity to meet their needs.

Enterprise High was named for the prime attribute that defined its structure. Students organized themselves around business ventures and worked in teams to make and sell products. Each team decided together how to invest their time and energy. Some built furniture. Others created artwork. Some began catering businesses and marketed food and services. Students split the profits based on the group's consensus of who deserved what percentage.

Each Enterprise High venture was staffed with one basic skill teacher and two or three enterprise teachers or paraprofessionals. Students learned math, reading, writing, and problem-solving skills in response to the business needs they encountered in the process of producing and selling items. They also learned to cooperate and resolve conflicts without violence. They learned to respect themselves, their accomplishments, and each other.

Working with at-risk students is a series of ups and downs, successes and setbacks. Heartbreak often alternates with celebration. Enterprise High was like that. Improved attendance was balanced by a teen pregnancy. Dope in the washroom muted the excitement of improved test scores.

And sometimes magic happened. A group of students was making dolls. Dolls with nylon stocking skins and cuddly nightgowns were especially popular at the time. In the woodshop, another team was making cradles for the dolls. They couldn't keep up with the Christmas orders.

During a break, a playful group of students crafted a full-sized, nylon stocking-skinned doll stuffed with cotton batting. Over time they gave her fiery red hair, a perky face, and fashionable (but not matching) earrings. They dressed her in the T-shirt of the season (REO Speedwagon) and a short denim skirt and finished her to look like . . . one of them.

The students named their friend "Clarissa" and began to dance with her during breaks. They spontaneously crafted a companion doll, Bill, to be Clarissa's boyfriend. Then Clarissa and Bill needed families. Families that looked like . . . theirs. There were aunts who raised them, half brothers, stray dogs, little brothers, cousins, grandparents who were not "blood related" but who were closer and more loving than any that might have been.

Around their two central characters emerged a circle of loving, troubled, struggling support persons. The creative staff seized the opportunity. Give them life, they suggested. Write about them. Who are they? Where did they come from? What was life like for them? What were prices like in their time? What was the world like? Reading, writing, research, history, geography, sociology, psychology, anatomy (they struggled to create life-size dolls that were self-standing and poseable, leading them to create internal skeletons of wire and wood modeled after the human skeleton) all came alive in Clarissa and Bill and their ragtag assemblage.

But what about enterprise? All this industry and creativity and production and no one was considering their marketability. How would they market these wonderful creations?

Brains began to storm. Cheap dates? Passengers in cars? Patients in waiting rooms? Clothing models in showrooms? There were lots of good ideas, but no commitment. There was no follow-through.

"What's the problem?" Julie Williams, their beloved teacher asked. One of the students was able to articulate their block, which until then had remained unconscious. "We can't sell just one to anybody. We have to sell them as a whole. We just can't . . . break up the family . . . ."

It was a profound moment. A hush fell over the room. The sadness was palpable. This group of ragtag dolls—freshly created with personalities, scars, trials, histories—this *family* could not be sold off, no matter what the price.

Their determination was tested. A dentist's office responded to their proposal to "never have an empty waiting room." The offer for one doll was $300. "No sale," was the response. A dress shop offered another $200 for a different character. "Sorry, no sale."

"Then what are we going to do with them?" Julie asked. "What can we do to make their creation feel completed and prized?" No one remembers whose idea it was, but the group pounced on it with unanimity. A wedding. Bill and Clarissa should get married. All the family members should attend and be seated on the appropriate sides of the altar as "friends of the bride" or "friends of the groom." Key family members should "stand up" for the bride and groom. The students would plan the wedding, build the altar, create the guest list, write the invitations, plan the menu, and prepare the food.

Some students made wedding clothing for the wedding parties. Others talked about ways to insure that Uncle Albert (no one's real uncle but married to the aunt [second marriage] who raised Clarissa) would not start drinking again at the reception.

Amy, another student, wrote the following history to be read at the ceremony:

THE SAGA OF THE TRASH CAN KIDS

Once upon a time there was a man who
collected junk.

He could see beauty in things that other people
thought were worthless.

One day he was going through a junk yard and
he came upon a Trash Can Kid.

This Kid appeared to be worthless to everyone
else, except to the man who collected junk.

The man took the Kid home and loved it. He
gave it a home and went out looking for other
Trash Can Kids.

The man took them all home. He gave them his
love. He gave them his heart.

And because he loved them, and because he gave
away his heart, they came to life!

And because of the life they had, they began to
love one another.

They even learned to love themselves.

And so we are here today to celebrate that love
as Clarissa and Bill carry it on into the future,
helping themselves stay alive
and others come alive
because of it.

The ceremony was brief and unspectacular. "The Saga of the Trash Can Kids" was brief and spectacular. The student who wrote it understood the real venture that had begun on that class break five months earlier. The students had created metaphors for their lives in the lives of these dolls. Amid the disconnectedness and interruptions of bloodlines, they had discovered something strong, something life giving, something life sustaining. That something was . . . a family. The kind of family that love can make. The kind of family that can be crafted from the connections we can make with others. The kind of family that gives life. The kind of family that is more valuable than money.♥

THIS IS BETTER THAN MEDITATION

Terry Wooten

The rain and the frogs singing
under an invisible full moon
were more interesting
than the 11 o'clock news.
Turned the porch light on.
Night crawlers were partying,
thousands of them
crawling all over
the cement and driveway,
getting it on,
braiding themselves in the grass.
I couldn't resist.
I put my raincoat on,
grabbed my flashlight
and waded out into the primitive.

Humming along with the frogs,
it's all come back to this.
Hunched over in the dark
with a flashlight
sneaking up on night crawlers
pouncing on them
stretched out in the rain.
I can feel their bodies recoil
like slippery nerves pulling back
quick into the wet earth.
My muddy fingers are strong
and know just where to pinch,
but I miss half of them.

Night crawlers didn't live in our yard
when I was a kid at home.
Dad would drive us
to the cemetery west of town
to catch the giant worms
in the dark warm rain.
We'd hunt through old and new graves
with our flashlights
like absentminded will-o-the-wisps
gathering night crawlers
in big coffee cans.
Later we'd trade 'em to the rivers
and lakes for fish.
I didn't realize how rich
we were then.♥

BRAVEHEART

Dottie Walters

When my children were young, they would often come crying to me with skinned knees or other real or imagined hurts. I would put my arms around them and tell them, "We must find the 'still' together. Take your right hand, put it under your left wrist, and gently place your fingers halfway across your arm, just above your left hand." They'd become so busy following my instructions they would stop crying and listen to what I said next.

"We have Scottish blood. Listen!" And I'd sing them the words my Scottish grandpa used to sing to me.

I hear the bagpipes coming!
I hear the drummers drumming,
Braveheart, my heart's drum, drumming
Scotland, the Brave!

"Your Scot's drums are always with you," I'd tell them. "As soon as you feel the beat, be still and think, 'What is the *best* thing—the *good* thing—to do to solve my problem?' You always have the ability to think what is right, in any emergency. Your Scot's Braveheart will give you the answer."

But that was a long time ago—a time before my husband had a strep infection of the blood and two strokes. Now, trying to do his job and mine in our business and making many trips to the hospital each day, I was stumbling. I felt lost.

One day I needed to leave a message for Michael, our grandson, who has a small rock band. The band's recording, loud and screaming, was on his answering machine. I hated to call him because I didn't like the sound, but I didn't want to let him know how awful I thought it was.

As I dialed his number, my heart was as heavy as the rock music I expected to hear. I braced myself for the blast of sound. But when the machine answered, I almost dropped the phone. Michael had changed the recording. Instead of heavy rock, I heard a real Scots' bagpipe band, skirling and swirling, beating out "Scotland, the Brave."

I got my grandson's message: *Braveheart, Nani, Braveheart.*♥

THE GIFT

Jane Sanders

My younger brother, Dean, married Judy, the love of his life in 1985. They waited to start a family until Dean got settled in his career and had finished a master's degree and they'd bought a house. By 1989, it was time. They were so excited about the prospect of having kids. And they had so much trouble.

One pregnancy ended in miscarriage within a month. Dean and Judy were devastated. Another pregnancy lasted only three months. Heartbreak once more. An ultrasound during yet another pregnancy discovered twins! Two tiny boys, Paul and Charles, named after their granddaddies, were born early, at five-and-a-half months. They lived only 30 minutes.

But Dean and Judy were persistent, and they were determined to have children. The minute the doctors said, "Okay, you can try again," they were pregnant. (Fortunately, fertility was never an issue.) And this time everything worked! On

Groundhog Day in 1992, my niece, Amy Marie, was born.

Later that year I went home for a family reunion, one of my all-time favorite events. I have six brothers and sisters, most of whom have families, so Dean and Judy's house was packed. We were all standing in the kitchen and dining room chatting when Dean took Amy upstairs to bed.

I was standing next to the counter where the intercom to the baby's room was located. Within a few minutes, over the din of the kitchen conversation, through the intercom, I heard the creak, creak, creak of the rocking chair as Dean rocked his infant daughter to sleep. And then, very softly, I heard something else. To the tune of the song, "Clementine," I heard my brother's voice crooning:

> Oh my daughter, oh my daughter, oh my daughter, Amy Marie.
> You're the answer to my prayers, oh my daughter, Amy Marie.
> Oh my daughter, oh my daughter, oh my daughter, Amy Marie.
> I'm your daddy and I love you, oh my daughter, Amy Marie.

My eyes filled with tears as I felt Dean's love for his long-awaited miracle baby. More important, I knew Amy could feel that love, too. And I knew the gift my brother was giving his infant daughter in that moment was as great as the gift she had given him with her birth.♥

SMALL THINGS

Rhoda D. Zagorsky
Assisted by Debra Zagorsky Agliano

It was a mother's nightmare come true. Our beautiful, 14-year-old daughter, Ellen, suddenly and mysteriously became ill with an assortment of severe physical problems. The Children's Hospital had no clue what was happening or how to help. What they did notice was a rapidly escalating curvature of her spine. So she was sent to the hospital's orthopedic department.

In this age of highly specialized medicine, the orthopedic doctors focused on her back problem. They performed major surgery, implanting steel rods to prevent her spine from further deterioration.

Since the underlying cause, the virus which causes Chronic Fatigue Syndrome, hadn't been identified or addressed, Ellen didn't recuperate. After two weeks in the hospital with no noticeable progress, she was sent home, unable to bear her own weight.

Our family had struggled to deal with the stressful months prior to Ellen's surgery. Now we had to face the possibility of her being a permanent invalid.

In the abstract, such crises of life present themselves in broad terms and seem overwhelming. In living out their reality, it's the small events and the concrete details of day-to-day coping that not only get us through but strengthen us.

Such a small event occurred for us shortly after Ellen's homecoming from what turned out to be only her first surgery.

A day arrived when it became clear that the task of washing her long, tangled hair couldn't be put off any longer. How to manage such a mundane task seemed daunting. She couldn't support herself in the shower, let alone climb into a tub. She had no muscle strength and was dead weight.

Our older daughter, Debra, and I brainstormed about how we might accomplish the hairwashing with Ellen still lying in bed. One of us spotted an old ironing board in a closet. Here was something strong enough to support Ellen's head, and it had holes which would allow water to drip through.

Debra and I removed the layers of padding from the ironing board and positioned it at the foot of Ellen's bed, adjusting it to the same height as the bed. Somehow we managed to drag Ellen onto it. Then we covered the mattress, the box spring, and the floor with green trash bags. We put absorbent towels everywhere else before setting a dishpan bucket under the holes of the ironing board. Debra and I put on bathing suits.

We began pouring cups of warm water over Ellen's scalp, massaging it with shampoo, while the three of us joked and laughed about the ridiculousness of what we were doing.

The unorthodox procedure produced "squeaky clean" hair for Ellen, but Debra and I looked as if we'd gotten caught in a heavy rainstorm. The mattress dried out, eventually.

Solving the dirty hair dilemma may seem like a "small thing," but it symbolized the process and the experience of coping together which helped us not only to get through Ellen's long ordeal but to grow in our love for and commitment to one another.

When Ellen finally recovered and was able, once again, to lead a normal life, it wasn't the only family victory.♥

TIME OUT FOR A LITTLE JOIE DE VIVRE

Joanna Slan

As we debarked Flight 819 from Paris, a reporter stuck a microphone in our faces. "Are you part of the $99 special trip? What did you buy?"

Excusez-moi, lady. You have the wrong idea. Despite what TWA's ad said about Paris, there is no finer place to shop than the Galleria, parking problems and all. However, if you want a gift to last a lifetime, bypass the sweaters, ties and toys. Instead, give your family a trip to Paris.

Don't get me wrong. David, my husband, is a retailer, for goodness sake, and we love "purchase therapy." But . . . do you really need another "thing"? I have 19—count 'em—19 sweaters and one body. Michael, my kid, has so many toys that we can't keep track of them.

Somehow, in our American atmosphere of affluence, we have confused "having" with "enjoying."

"Are We Having Fun, Yet?" is the title of a program I present as a professional speaker and trainer. The program includes a handout that asks people what they do for fun. Gee, talk about your tough questions. People will sit and stare at the paper for 15 minutes without a clue. One woman fell to work quickly and filled the entire sheet of paper with one word: eat.

Seems that life has become a spectator sport. Consuming has replaced experiencing, and we are emptier and sadder as a result.

Many years ago, a wise woman told me, "When our children came along, my husband and I decided to invest in experiences instead of in things."

That's why, with five hours' notice last Thursday, we packed three carry-on bags, picked up five-year-old Michael from Montessori school, and boarded the TWA flight for a 48-hour trip to Paris.

Yes, we did make a few purchases: 16 postcards, a sweatshirt, and a teddy bear. But let me tell you what we really bought.

I "bought" the pleasure of holding my son's hand as he went up and down on a white carousel horse with a real horsehair tail. As we made lazy circles, the lights of Paris were shining all around us through the misty rain. I whispered in my son's ear, "Make a picture in your mind so you always remember." Once a revolution, my husband would wave and smile from beneath his Chicago Bears hat.

We "bought" a look at Paris from a glass elevator car climbing our way up, up, up through the fog to the second level of the Eiffel Tower.

There the two-inch-thick cables strained to haul us to an observation deck. Below us, the rain-sliced city twinkled like a child's Lite Brite set.

We "bought" a song from an organ-grinder as he turned the crank on a music box while his little dog and cat slept next to him on a doll's bed. We saw the building where Chopin died, the place where Francois Mitterrand works, and the prison where Marie Antoinette awaited the slice of the guillotine.

Yes, what we really bought was a lifetime of memories. For all time, we will own a vision of Paris dressed for Christmas with short-needled pine trees sporting huge metallic bows, balls, and lights. When Michael is grown, I will remind him how we skipped through Metro tunnels singing "Frosty the Snowman." David and I will recall a romantic dinner for two where the waiter kept serving me chocolate, chocolate, and more chocolate.

Before we left the City of Light, Paris gave me a gift. We were wandering down the Rue de Rivoli window shopping. David was carrying Michael because jet lag had finally caught up with our indefatigable little boy. A motorcyclist drove up behind me and said, "Oooo-la-la." Then he turned to my husband and said, "You take the baby. I'll take the mama." With that, he roared off into the sunset.

That did more for my 41-year-old heart than chocolate, carousels, and a whole drawer full of Wonder-Bras.

No, we didn't buy a lot in Paris, and I'm not at all disappointed. All those "things" we own, own us. Experiences are the stuff life is made of. You can't claim them at customs; you can't pack them or wrap them, and they will fit you the rest of your days. My life is richer than it was a few days ago with moments I could only imagine.

The next time you see a weekend special from TWA, don't just dream about it. Go for it. And I'll see you on the plane.♥

(Reprinted from the December 15, 1994, St. Louis Post-Dispatch)

THE WIZARDS OF NATIONS CREEK*

Ben Burton

To a real scientist, certain beliefs, myths, and theories just scream out to be investigated.

"The world is flat."

"Man can't fly."

"Elvis is dead."

"Cats always land on their feet" cried out just that way to my brother Len and me. "Always lands on his feet." That seemed so illogical. Take the word *always*. Always is never always, not one thing is always. Could a cat have the corner on always?

Len and I set out to give this theory a proper scientific challenge. We would let the cats fall where they would, to use a little laboratory humor.

*In no way do we recommend, defend, or make light of the treatment of Lindbergh or any other animal as reported here. We earnestly hope that we all, adults and children alike, are more enlightened and sensitive today than some of us were when we were children.

If you know anything at all about science, you know it requires a systematic approach. Oh, we had done some random cat tossing, and the old theory seemed to hold up. We never felt it necessary to get into the heavy stuff, things like the cat juggling we had heard about from our cousin who had once visited some of the dens of iniquity in Mexico.

What we needed was a plan—a series of tests to find out once and for all if cats did indeed always land on their feet. Our minds were more than open, and then some. We surely did not want or intend to be cruel, but obviously we needed the help of a cat. Fortunately, we had Lindbergh, a long-time but generally non-participating member of the family. He was the real hero of this story.

Lindbergh was not particularly cooperative, but he was easy to catch and forgiving—or had a short memory. And he only left home at night. All this was good because the experiments were to last several days. We decided that three experiments would validate or invalidate the widely-held belief about a cat's sense of balance.

The experiments were to be planned and conducted in an orderly manner. All results were to be observed and recorded until we reached a "provable and replicable conclusion." (Len copied that part out of a book.) We were determined not to fail.

The story is best told in our own records, that is from our lab notes (actually the barn, but who would ever put any faith in barn notes?):

Experiment Number 1

Hypothesis: The cat's secret lies in his good eyesight and ability to locate the ground from any posture.

Test: Blindfold the subject, turn him on his back, and drop from a high place.

Results: Failure. Lindbergh unruly and uncooperative after two hours of attempting to blindfold. Apparently fails to understand his potential place in history.

Ancillary findings: Cats have practically no forehead.

Experiment Number 2

Hypothesis: The cat's uncanny balance is a product of his acute hearing.

Test: Stuff cotton into the cat's ears until he sits perfectly still even when the dog barks. Toss into the air and observe landing.

Results: Incomplete and inconclusive. Cats are sensitive about ears. Lindbergh unusually violent. Scratched friendly lab assistant (me). Removed cotton as fast as inserted. Idea to restrain subject's hands and feet abandoned as impractical. It would make heart of the experiment—the landing— awkward and meaningless.

For sale: Two pairs of paw cuffs. Barely used.

Experiment Number 3

Hypothesis: The cat's ability to land on his feet results from his intelligence and/or rapid processing of visual and oral data.

Test: Get the cat drunk and drop from a high place. Two methods of getting Lindbergh drunk considered. (1) Fermented pokeberry juice. Little data available on amount of pokeberry juice needed. (2) Spin the cat around until he's drunk. We had learned in a yard game that running around in several tight circles with forehead resting on a hoe handle could make one lose all one's sense of balance and direction. No luck at all in getting Lindbergh to run around hoe handle even after we cut one down to his size: 4 1/8", short oval. Then, just as we began to despair, the break came. So much of good science is accidental, like penicillin, gravity, barbecue, etc.

Suddenly one of us remembered that we once got drunk spinning around on the bag swing. From there it was a short distance for two young wizards to design and make a harness for Lindbergh and swing him from the hay lift in the barn and spin him around until he was good and drunk.

Results: Victory! Just like his namesake, Lindbergh made history! On the trip down from the barn loft, Lindbergh squirmed instinctively to get his feet into the down position. In his drunken condition some error was inevitable. A miscalculation of 180 degrees was unexpected. Lindbergh came in flat on his back. Happy to report no apparent injury from the landing.

The hero did bang himself up superficially when he sprang up and sprinted full speed into the side of the barn. Just happy, I guess. Left area listing severely to port and humming "Bird in a Gilded Cage."

From those crude notes, one gets little feel for the gratification the scientist enjoys from knowing that he has contributed. No rewards, no honors, no wealth or acclaim come close to matching the feeling one has knowing that he has unearthed the truth.

As for Lindbergh, he recovered to live many more proud years. While he was more stand-offish than ever and never spoke to Len and me again, we know he gets the same thrill we do from seeing in some of the more responsible, if unsung, journals the truth: "Cats *almost* always land on their feet." The truth makes us free!♥

THE STUMP

Avril Johannes

Oh, I've seen that old stump before!
A flash of memory. You and I hunting together. Me doing the bird-dogging, searching through the brush and trees for a moose. "There!" I call to you. Then, "No! Don't shoot!" It's that same old wild stump, another year older, still causing an instant surge of adrenaline, like last year and the years before. Remember how we laughed.

There is a difference now. You are no longer here with me. This is not a hunting trip for the family meat. This is a return to a place we called home, a venture to find me, and remember us.

So, here I am once again, and here is the same island, the same wild stump. Strange how nothing has changed. It is as I remember. Only I have changed. The peace, quiet, and beauty are as they were. The wolf tracks are there. Maybe not the same wolves, maybe different beavers in the pond, maybe the same family of squirrels making piles of empty pine cone petals. It is all so familiar.

But this time I am a visitor, though not a stranger. This time I will observe differently, see through eyes that look into the past, not the present. That will change, I know. I will come to the present and, hopefully, glimpse a course for the future.

You taught me the immense importance of saying "I love you." In my mind's eye I see the firelight flickering on the polished logs of the home we built. My inner ear hears the music softly playing in the background and your voice, saying, "Any time we have to be apart, let the last thing we say to each other be, 'I love you.' I know we won't always feel like it, but however we feel on the surface, underneath we know we do love each other."

The children followed our example, even when they left for school each day. At times we could tell they would rather not have said it, might even have preferred saying something to the contrary as they slammed their way out of the door.

When you became ill and went to the hospital, the doctor told me you would not be coming home. He said I should tell you anything I wanted you to know. So many thoughts: *Don't leave me. Stay.* So many plans. *Forty-four is too young to die. I can't do it alone. What about the children? God, don't take him. Why us?* Selfish thoughts, every one of them.

Pulling myself together, I returned to the intensive care unit. Trying to smile to cover my breaking heart and destroyed world, I sat holding your hand. We talked as you drifted in and out of consciousness. You asked me to go home and get some rest.

I didn't want to leave. You didn't want me to stay. Our last hug. One more chance to tell you how much I love you. One last time to hear you whisper, "I love you, also."

In the years you have been gone, I found I have capabilities I was not aware of. You always had faith in me, but I always looked to you for strength and advice. For so long, I wandered. I roamed from room to room, inside to outside, and back. Such a lost being. I didn't know what I was looking for, but it must have been your companionship, your influence. You. We shared everything: love, children, time, sickness, health, money, lack of money, play, gladness and sadness. We shared our innermost thoughts, our hopes, dreams, fears, and desires. We knew each other as well as two people sharing a life are able to.

This island and I have a lot in common. We have both gained new growth. People have come and gone in our lives, some leaving tracks that will remain forever, some taking parts and pieces, some leaving treasures and some, debris.

This old stump and I have a commonality, too. Its basic structure has not changed. It stands alone quite strong against the forces that be. It is there to be leaned upon for support, if needed.

Somehow, even in your absence you give me strength. Because of you and your belief in me, I am able to do what is necessary each day. I try to stand tall in a manner I feel you would approve. Oh, I still have my fears, lots of old, annoying habits, ghosts of years gone by and no real plans for the future. But for whatever reason, I feel peaceful by this old, wild stump. And tomorrow is another day.

Wherever you are, I love you.♥

WATCHING STARS

Joe Lamancusa

When my sons were growing up, it wasn't unusual, on a clear, cloudless night, to feel one of them tugging at my arm. I'd look down into his small, innocent face, and he would ask if we could go outside and watch for satellites. Gathering pillow and blanket, we would go out on our back deck, open a recliner chair, and stretch out on it. My son on my chest, I'd cover us both with the blanket, and we would look up into the sky.

We played a game to see who would be the first to spot a moving satellite. While we watched, I would talk about what the moving light really was, how it got there, and where it was going. I'd tell him about the visible constellations and teach him how to distinguish between a satellite and an airplane.

Suddenly he would spot a moving pinpoint of light and scream, "There's one!" A feeling of accomplishment would settle over him like the cool night air, and we would remain out for a while longer, warm and close under the blanket, enjoying just being together.♥

CUTTING EDGES AND GIFTS

Bill Decker

"It's not okay to threaten your little sister with a knife."

Those were my words as I walked out of my older daughter's bedroom. My tone was firm, yet not blaming. My words were clear, and limits were stated.

I was doing everything right. Why was I shaking? Why did I feel so helpless? Why was I so scared? How did we get to this place? How could this be happening in *my* family?

Both of our daughters were adopted from Thailand. We adopted the second when she was about 12. She had lived since infancy in an orphanage outside of Bangkok. Our first daughter was 5 when her big sister moved in.

As our new daughter learned English, she slowly revealed stories of her life. In her innocence, she told us tales of great caring mixed with horrors that no child should have to endure. She was a survivor. She was not ready for the dynamics and intimacies of a family.

From day one she thought her sister was spoiled beyond belief. Why didn't we beat her when she did something wrong? What was the big deal with just losing privileges? She decided to take things into her own hands. But threatening with knives and cleavers is just not acceptable in our family.

As I left her room, her last words rang in my ears: "I kill you all tonight!"

Downstairs, my wife was on the phone with our daughter's counselor. She told us that if we were afraid to sleep in our own home we needed to do something and suggested having her committed to the adolescent psych unit for evaluation. She said we'd be sending a very concrete message about what is acceptable behavior and what is not.

Soon I found myself bear-hugging, restraining, and carrying down the stairs an 85-pound snarling, kicking, terrified ball of fury. She bit my hand until it bled. My wife drove the van.

I was scared. I was furious. I was in a movie. How could this be happening in *my* family?

The first four weeks she was in the hospital she refused to talk with or even look at us. Her whole attitude, the attitude of a survivor, was that *we* were wrong. It was *our* fault. *We* were the bad ones doing this to her. *We* needed to change.

Since the adoption had not been finalized, we struggled over whether to proceed or not. If she was not willing to take responsibility for her actions, if she would not work on communicating or developing self-awareness, would it be safe to take her back into our family? Was she so damaged by her early life experiences that "normal" family life was impossible for her? Were we willing to restructure our life to become a therapeutic community for her if she would not or could not change?

The discussions, the decisions, the emotions were grueling and gut-wrenching.

We decided to terminate the adoption.

The international adoption agency was contacted. They purchased the tickets. The flights were arranged. Our daughter's possessions were boxed up and ready to go. I was travelling on business when my wife went to tell her.

The next day we both went to visit her. We found a child so dejected she looked like her bones had been pulled out. She dragged her long black hair over her face to hide the fact that she'd been crying for the past 24 hours. She gave us the good-bye gifts she had spent the day making for us.

With the prodding of her counselor, she parted her hair and, avoiding eye contact, said, "I sorry. I not do again." A small step. A huge step. The words—what did they mean to her? Did she understand them, or was she just mouthing them?

We decided to trust. We terminated the termination. But it took two more weeks before we were confident enough to bring her home. To try again.

It has been four years since we made that decision. It has taken tremendous amounts of work: hours of talking, strict limits with consistent consequences, blood, sweat, tears, and help from extended family, counselors, teachers, and friends. But there have also been pleasant surprises and celebrations. In that four years our daughter's delightfulness and sweet spirit have often shined forth. They complement her survival skills.

Recently she was talking with me about boys. She was sharing a depth of self-awareness I had doubted she'd ever be able to achieve or express. I wondered if she could reflect with equal self-awareness on her time in the hospital. I asked her. She replied, with a simplicity of language that achieved elegance, "It was good, Dad. I begin change." My eyes teared up. Waves of relief, a relaxation, a satisfaction washed over me. A guilt I had not even known I was carrying eased.

Where else but in the family do we get so many opportunities to go through the crucible—so many chances to co-create miracles?♥

THE LAMANCUSA SPAGHETTI RITUAL

Joe Lamancusa, Jr.
Age 17

After a long, tiring day at school listening to monotone teachers talk about the square root of x and the correct usage of a participial phrase, nothing is more welcome to me when I arrive home than the smell of a fresh pot of Mom's special spaghetti sauce simmering on the stove. As the aroma enters my nostrils, I feel all the hassles of the day drifting away until all that remains in my mind is the thought of consuming mass quantities of delicious spaghetti.

It is widely known in our house that it takes many hours of careful preparation to make the sauce, so that every time we're blessed with it for dinner I feel a special love coming from the spaghetti, a love that signifies my mom's effort in making our dinner the very best it can be. The meal has a magical cleansing effect. While I'm eating, everything else seems insignificant by comparison.

There is also a lot of history behind my mom's sauce. She got the recipe from my grandmother, who is 100 percent Sicilian and still makes it for most of the family gatherings. My grandma learned the recipe from her mother, who lived the first quarter of her life in Sicily.

Eating my mom's spaghetti temporarily suspends me in time. It's like having my grandmother, and even her ancestors, cook for me.♥

A MATTER OF LIFE AND DEPTH

Joe Kogel

I was diagnosed with malignant melanoma on October 28, 1981. I was 25 years old. Melanoma is a form of skin cancer. It's the kind most likely to kill you.

I wasn't given any statistics. No haunting, "You have three months left to live, Mr. Kogel." I was told that while the tumor was still only in the skin, it was a deep lesion.

A native of New Jersey, I had just graduated from college in a small town in southern Oregon. I was working as a sportswriter for the *Daily Tidings*, a newspaper in Ashland. My girlfriend had recently moved to Berkeley, and we were trying to make the relationship work long distance. It wasn't.

I wept often out of a pure joy that I was alive; I had only been diagnosed, I hadn't been buried. I wept for all the incompleteness in my life: the aborted love affairs, the unspoken feelings, the unrealized dreams of writing and performing and marrying.

The intensity of my desire to live seemed to have earned me a spot on the hotline to God. I suspect my mother also had something to do with my getting through. From the moment of diagnosis, my mother began stuffing the cosmic ballot box with her prayers, as though she'd scribbled "Save Joe Kogel" on thousands of tiny scraps of paper.

The image I have is of God arising one morning from her futon, putting the coffee on, and sitting down to open the morning prayers.

First slip of paper: "Save Joe Kogel." Okay.

Next slip: "Save . . . Joe Kogel."

Warily she unfolds the third prayer of the morning: "Save Joe . . . " Okay, you win; who *is* Joe Kogel?! The phone rings. It's God's secretary. "I have a call for you on line one."

"Don't tell me," God says, no stranger to these wild coincidences. "Joe Kogel?"

A year-and-a-half after my diagnosis, I assembled my writings in the form of an autobiographical one-man show called "Stories You've Never Heard Before." The show chronicled a period from before my birth when my grandfather committed suicide during the Depression through my diagnosis of cancer. It dealt with growing up, falling in love, and transforming different kinds of pain into something useful and—in some cases— something beautiful. I wanted to present ideas through stories from my own life. The bottom line was simply that an appreciation of the preciousness of life could be a means to living more gracefully and, as a natural course, dying more gracefully whenever that time comes, be it a result of cancer or of getting run over by the number 52 bus in the middle of an otherwise harmless Thursday afternoon.

Sponsored by colleges and community arts councils, "Stories" toured the Northwest. I arranged all my own bookings, spent many nights on living room floors, and continued to refine my craft.

But, like many new businesses, mine was low on capital and needed help. My mother was now *actually* scribbling "Joe Kogel," but the slips of paper had printed on them "Pay to the order of" before my name. My mother's money kept me afloat the first few years of the new business venture, although autobiographical storytelling was not the career she had in mind for me, I'm certain. But she believed, as I did, that I was doing what I needed to do to maximize my immune system's strength. That my mother is not a wealthy woman made her gift all the more meaningful.

My new show, "Life and Depth," is not about defeating a foe called cancer. My health, instead, seems to be the by-product of a life lived full-bore. I set out to forgive myself and others totally. I set out to obey the passions of my art. I chose work as my talisman. As a by-product of these choices, I found myself healing.

I also found myself getting married and moving back East from the West Coast, where I'd lived my entire adult life. My wife (a native of Boston) and I returned East for the same reason we left: because our families were there. Uprooting one's life from a community of 20 years at the age of 35 is not as difficult as getting cancer. But had I never gotten cancer, I never would have returned East.

Cancer taught me about the nature of mortality—my own and that of people I love. My mother, who gave me life, saved my life by believing in me and showing it in every way possible. What she gave me, she gave freely. I had no obligation to repay her. She didn't save my life so I would move East when I recovered. She saved my life because that is what there was to do.

That's why my wife and I moved East. Because the tug of family never diminished over 3,000 miles and two decades. If anything, it got stronger. The tug had some obligation in it—maybe one part per thousand. The other 999 had to do with a sense of completion—of being nearby as our parents aged and died. As our nieces and nephews matured, they would have another pole to go to —an Aunt Susan and Uncle Joe to run to when the heat at home became too much.

As we contemplated starting our own family, we wanted to know that our children would truly know their roots—our roots. And not from snapshots and annual visits. We wanted to complete the circle. We wanted to face what we'd run from.

We wanted to come home.♥

II.

FATHERS

"IF YOU LOVE ME, SAY *THAT!*"

Mitch Anthony

Jerry couldn't forget the snowy, winter day that his first-born son almost had a serious accident. Jeff was in his first year of driving, which made Jerry nervous to begin with. The close call with disaster only heightened his anxiety.

One day following the near-accident, Jeff told his father he was getting ready to leave the house.

"Drive carefully, now!" Jerry warned.

Jeff turned to his father with a look of chagrin and asked, "Why do you always say that?"

"Say what?"

"'Drive carefully.' It's like you don't trust me driving."

"No, son, that's not it at all," Jerry explained. "It's just my way of saying, 'I love you.'"

"Well, Dad, if you want to say you love me, say *that!*" Jeff said. "That way I can't mix up the message."

"But . . . " Jerry hesitated. "What if your friends are here with you? If I say 'I love you,' you might get embarrassed."

"In that case, Dad, when you're saying good-bye, just put your hand near your heart, and I'll do the same," Jeff offered.

Jerry was touched that his son wanted, as badly as he, to express his love. "You've got a deal," he said.

A few days later, Jeff was getting ready to leave again, this time with a friend. "Can I have the keys, Dad?" he asked his father.

"Sure," Jerry answered. "Where are you headed?"

"Downtown."

Jerry tossed him the keys. "Jeff," he said, pausing before adding, "have a great time." He subtly placed his hand near his heart. Jeff did the same. "Sure, Dad," he said.

Jerry winked.

Jeff walked back to his father and whispered, "Winks weren't a part of the deal." Jerry was slightly taken aback.

Jeff headed for the door. "Okay, Dad, see 'ya," he said. Just before he shut the door, he turned back—and winked.♥

HAIL! THE BOY KING

Ben Burton

At the lake I saw a young daddy teaching his kids to fish. Just a boy, really, but in the eyes of his young children, a king! The scene flashed me back in time to another young father out with his children. For I, too, was once a boy king.

For a moment I envied the young father this priceless time and privilege—a time like this when my children knew that I knew it all, that I could do anything and everything. What a crowning feeling! But what an obligation! Like this boy, I was unaware then of the latter.

How can any father misuse these defining moments in his children's lives? For them, even the tiniest fish, a trophy; even the weakest and most selfish father, a king. Isn't this young man conscious that he is weaving lifetimes here? His every attitude a warp; his every inflection a woof. No, I conclude, the boy/man is unaware of this greater role.

Trouble is, this young father, though "king" to his children, still has a lot of boy in himself; a boy seeking his own trophy, hunting his own crown. Nevertheless, he is molding his children's memories and attitudes and lives—and their own parenting skills—right now.

I decide that I don't envy the young father his imposing responsibility after all—nor begrudge him his numbness to it. Not knowing that he isn't yet up to this awesome job, the boy is eager to keep at it. All the while, his children see him as the best king ever.

Nature is merciful that way; compensating both ends of the budding parent-child relationship. Patient, too.

This boy/king will need much practice and faithfulness. And luck. Didn't we all? The key is that he, with his boundless exuberance, is here, this day, with his children. And that alone is a beautiful start.♥

DADDY'S GIFT

Shirley D. Garrett

It's been a tough day, depleting me of energy, enthusiasm, and confidence. Looking for a way to recharge, I wander outdoors and straddle my old but functional bicycle. It's nothing fancy but it's just the right vehicle to free a bound spirit.

Pedalling up the driveway, my body effortlessly controlling the movement of the bike, I recall my favorite family story and begin replaying it in my mind. It's a very old story—one I've heard countless times over the past 40 years, one that's told at every family gathering without fail.

It was 1955, on the Eve of the first real Christmas that I and my sister, Mary, ever had, and Daddy was determined that his two new daughters would find it filled with love and joy.

I was four, Mary was two, and the entire process of our "coming to live with" Daddy, Mama, and Lamar took place without Daddy's ever laying eyes on us. When asked how he could adopt two children sight unseen, Daddy would answer, "It doesn't matter to me what they look like. If they need a home, we want 'em."

On the day of our arrival, the blue Dodge pulled into the yard holding Mary and me, our brothers, and the two new mothers. (A second family was adopting our brothers.) Daddy had chosen to stay home with Lamar, who was having "soon-to-be-older-brother" jitters.

Our first two months with our new family were joyful, but expensive. We brought with us a lot of "needs": tonsils that needed removing, medications that needed to be taken, clothes that needed to be obtained. Our greatest need was for emotional support and reassurance that this was indeed our home—for life.

The townspeople pitched in: neighbors hosted a "children's shower," the local pharmacist donated the required medications, someone provided a new tricycle for Santa to bring Mary. As Christmas approached, Daddy's sister, Florice, secretly put the finishing touches on a set of matching mother-and-daughter dresses that Daddy knew would leave Mama in tears. Lamar, at 14, was old enough to help plan the details of how Santa would deliver the new baby dolls, the blocks that had been fashioned in the shop from leftover bits of wood, and the special stocking stuffer.

Everything seemed to be in order for a wonderful Christmas celebration, yet Daddy was restless. He couldn't forget a small blue bicycle "Santa" had access to for ten dollars. He and Mama agreed they had spent enough for the time being. After all, there was always the chance our birth parents would reclaim us—a right they could exercise for up to a year.

Daddy paced and thought—and thought and paced. He sensed that I had the most profound of the scars from our past. I was afraid of the dark, afraid of enclosed spaces, even afraid to go to the bathroom alone. In fact, I couldn't speak an intelligible sentence and often needed Mary to interpret for me.

As dusk began to fall, Daddy told Mama he had one last errand to run. When he returned home a short time later with the bicycle (complete with training wheels), he declared, "Heck, if they take Shirley back, they can take the bicycle, too."

On Christmas morning my eyes grew wide as I beheld the beautiful blue bicycle. Daddy quickly recognized that I didn't need the training wheels after all and removed them. As I began to pedal, he released his hold on the bike, sending me off for the first time on the road to freedom. But even as he let me go, he ran alongside me, there to help if I wavered too far off course.

As I ride now, I remember that first send-off and the many more that came later. Whether I was attending my first day of school, learning to drive, heading off to college, or taking my first job, Daddy's parenting style was consistent. He provided me with a way to soar, but the "training wheels" of his love and guidance were always there beside me, ready to support and redirect me if I needed them.

Entering a straightaway, I rediscover my center of balance, release the handlebars, and lift my hands to the sky in jubilant celebration.♥

CHOOSING TO STAND TALL

Patricia Ball

I was my current height—5 feet 11 inches—at the age of 13. I was also very gangly. It took all my powers of concentration to make my head, arms, and legs coordinate successfully.

Like so many young people who sprout to great heights at an early age, I was very self-conscious. I thought that if I slouched—tried to round my shoulders and make myself smaller—people wouldn't notice how tall I was.

My father noticed, and one day he said to me, "If you're trying to hide your height, slouching won't work. Because you're tall, when you enter a room people will notice you. That's a given fact. All poor posture does is call more attention to you. As I see it, you have two choices. One, you can go ahead and slouch. People will notice and feel sorry about your lack of confidence. Two, you can stand with excellent posture. Then people will see a regal-looking, self-assured, statuesque young woman."

That was a powerful speech—one I remember word-for-word to this day. After that, "choice" became a very important word for me.

I took my dad's comments to heart. I spent a lot of time thinking about what he had said. I began practicing good posture, I worked to develop a positive attitude, and I became interested in building sound self-esteem.

It didn't take long to discover my father was right. If I walk into a room as if I own it, people do notice, but in a complimentary way. The more positive feedback I get, the more positive I feel about myself—and the taller I stand.

Great advice, Dad.♥

TO DAD–IN APPRECIATION

Spencer Kagan

Dear Dad,

Although you know that I am appreciative of the ways in which you have been an extraordinary provider, I haven't ever taken the time to put my feelings into a letter.

I am a mind person, and as I grew up it would have been very easy for me to lose touch with concrete reality. Partially because of who you are and partially because you sensed a need for greater balance in my life, over the years you insisted on my involvement in the physical: baseball, weight lifting, judo, fishing, hunting, trap and target shooting. I was not always the most enthusiastic, willing (or, at the time, appreciative) partner, but your encouragement and insistence were very good for me.

Now, as I look back, I am *very* appreciative. My life is fuller and more balanced because of you. The work I did building the ranch has its roots in your teaching me as a six-year-old how to rewire an electrical plug. The joy I had last night taking the kids out to hit baseballs and race miniature cars can be traced back to your getting up early each morning and taking the time before work to swing the baseball bolo for me in the front yard on Sarah Street. The time and care you took to show me how to tie a hook on a line, and how to hold a gun, has translated for years now into enjoyment for me and my sons. Last night I was working with Carlos on his batting stance and found myself being you, saying things like "plant your back foot" and "try to drive the bat *through* the ball."

What you have given me is ongoing; I receive from those experiences every day. I pass them along. And I am far more grateful than words can say.

I am especially appreciative because I know that much of what you gave did not come easily. You had to create "fatherhood" and "family" out of whole cloth. It is a simple thing for a father to hug and hold a kid, or pitch baseballs to him, or teach those new words each day if that father has been hugged and held and pitched to and taught by his own father. It is much harder to give what you have never received. Easy it is to follow a trail well trod; far more difficult and noble to blaze a new trail to follow a deeper instinct toward a new territory never seen, sensed only by the heart.

You had to reach deeper than most to find the direction and strength to lead our family. What for others would have been familiar territory, for you was unfamiliar. I am thankful you had the wisdom and courage and strength of instinct to lead us to this loving place. Today it is easier for me to hug my boys than it was for you to hug me, and for them it will be the most natural thing in the world. As they pick up and hug and hold their kids, they won't even think about it, but I will be watching—and I will know those hugs were won with difficulty by a man who had the strength to give his son what he was never given.

My spoken and written vocabulary is richer today because years ago you insisted on "three new words a day" at the breakfast table. My career and life work have had as much success as they have because you modeled a love of learning and pursuit of excellence. My *life vocabulary* is immeasurably richer because you dared to learn an unfamiliar language—and pass it on to me.

The language of family and of love that you, with difficulty, learned and modeled will continue to be spoken by future generations of Kagans long after you and I are gone.

I am appreciative of all the love you have given, and the love it continues to generate.

Your son, Spencer♥

THE FAMILY INTERSECTION

Miles McCall

Traffic signal rules are simple. Red means stop. Yellow means proceed with caution, prepared to stop. Green means go, after you look in all other directions.

If we all know the rules, then why do we have so many accidents? Because people don't pay attention or they choose to break them.

When a traffic accident occurs, progress is halted, damage is done, and people are often hurt. The same is true when two people approach each other in opposing psychological directions (known as "conflict"). When we don't pay attention to the obvious signals, an accident occurs, progress is halted, damage is done, and people are hurt.

I really began to understand this process after my mom passed away at the young age of 51. I was left to deal with Dad, a hard-headed, non-listening, chemical-dependent teenager in a 51-year-old body. Within three months after we buried my mom, Dad remarried. She was a waitress from the local bar, determined to take advantage of his emotional and financial state, neither of which was particularly stable.

Within ten months after their marriage, thanks to a couple of gambling trips and Dad's new wife's bingo addiction, the insurance money was gone and the reality of a "dry well" began to set in. Soon Wife Number 2 was gone, but not officially divorced, and "live-in" Wife Number 3 arrived.

Dad and I had numerous conflicts during this time. Neither of us paid attention to the signals, and there were no rules. Accidents occurred, progress was halted, damage was done, and people got hurt. It was while I was sitting in the middle of that accident of life that I realized the important role that rules and signals play in managing conflict and negotiating confrontation successfully.

It was three years after Mom's death that I finally learned the lesson and made the rules.

I called my dad and told him I wanted to come see him. There were things I needed to say to him. I told him that I would confront him on his turf, face to face, but the rule was that he could not say anything back to me. No yelling, no questions, no verbal response until he took some time to cool down and think about the things I said. I told him that when I was through, I would just drive away and he had to wait two full weeks before he responded to me in any way.

"Fine, smart college boy. You just bring it on, Bud," he responded from the other end of the line in his usual rough cowboy manner. I hung up the phone and spent the next five hours outlining my thoughts and comments. I rehearsed the key content points with my wife, getting her feedback and input. I looked through piles of paperwork, getting specific dates and information to increase my effectiveness in convincing my dad that he should have listened more to my brother and me over the past three years.

By 7:30 the next morning I had made the two-hour drive to where he lived and was knocking on his door.

Pop came out and we visited for a few minutes over coffee. Then I asked him if he was ready to listen. He nodded. I picked up my legal notepad with some six pages of notes. Over the course of the next two hours I proceeded down my list. Each time he attempted to interrupt I cut him off, shut him up, reminded him of the rules, and probably raised his blood pressure another notch. I finished my list and felt good! As I drove away, I saw him in my rearview mirror. He looked like a bulldog with his lip poked out, face bright red from anger, chest bowed out ready to fight. I think if he could have caught me he would have ripped my heart out.

Two weeks later I had forgotten our little confrontation. Then, at 6:15 one morning, there was a knock on my front door. I opened it to find my dad standing there with an unusual look of determination in his eyes. He said, "Sit down, boy, and listen. You know the rules; you made 'em. No interrupting, no questions. Just listen." He pulled out his legal pad with what looked like at least ten pages of notes. For the first time in my life he actually seemed to be more organized than I. For the next three hours he systematically went through his list, responding to each of my comments from our previous meeting. As he drove away after finishing, he looked back at me. I felt red as fire, veins bulging from the side of my head, and if it hadn't been illegal I would have run him down!

Over the next 18 months my dad and I continued to play the "rule" game. Eventually we cut the time between confrontations down to one week, then one day. At the end we narrowed it to just a few minutes. The anger decreased and became frustration, sadness, and finally respect. We tackled each and every issue we had between us while constantly referring to the rules to control flow. Finally we began to yield to the right of way, proceed with caution, and, occasionally, give each other the green light.

After a long weekend of deer hunting together, we stood at the gate of the deer lease in conversation. Dad told me how pleased he was that we had learned to work through our differences and how he appreciated my rules— how they had taught him to "control the flow." With a parting hug he said, "Thanks. I love you, son," and we drove off in opposite directions.

The next morning, at 8:05, I received a call at work. My dad had died of a stroke, almost instantaneously. My grief at losing him was mixed with gratitude that before his death we had learned to use the rules that allowed us to resolve our conflicts and negotiate a hazardous family intersection safely and with respect.♥

CHOOSING WHO WE ARE

Naomi Rhode

"Because you are our very cherished daughter, I made a special gift for you," my father told me during his presentation ceremony the night before I left home to go to camp for the first time. "I want you to accept this gift as a very special sign of our love. When you look at it, remember who you are."

Even though I was only 12, I knew that in our family "remembering who you are" meant we were children of wonderful people with great ancestors of deep spiritual faith.

After his speech of affirmation, my dad presented me with a piece of wood he had carved and painted into the shape of an animal that resembled a penguin. He named the carving Goofus.

The next day I went to camp with Goofus in my suitcase as a reminder that I was a special person. Raised in an atmosphere of high trust and low fear, I was assured of my parents' confidence in me to make good choices.

While at camp I met a 14-year-old boy with whom I became so enraptured that I gave him Goofus. As an adult I don't understand that choice, but as a child it made perfect sense.

"Dad, I gave Goofus away to the boy I am going to marry," I proudly explained when I got home.

Dad's response was classic: "He must be a very special person."

Rather than degrading, disciplining, or reprimanding his 12-year-old daughter for thinking so little of his gift, he accepted my choice. Unfortunately, Dad died a year later, so he didn't live long enough to experience the reality of his statement. The boy's name was Jim Rhode, and seven years later I married him. We kept Goofus as a reminder of my dad's confidence in my ability to make the right choices.♥

TRACTOR POWER

John R. Ramsey

My father spent the first 20 years of his life trying to get off the farm—and the last 20 trying to get back. When I realized just how important it was to him to reconnect with his farm roots, I vowed to help him do it.

Dad left the farm when he was 17. Desperate to leave Kentucky and see the world, he enlisted in the U.S. Air Force. He served 21 years and then took a government job working in the Civil Service Engineering Center. In the meantime, he had married and he and my mother had begun raising a family which eventually included five sons.

As I watched my father age over the years, it became clear that what he'd like most was to trade his office cubicle for a small garden spot. He couldn't wait to lay his briefcase down and pick up a shovel. Hard as it was to believe, this man who had walked the halls of the Pentagon would rather walk down a row of corn and feel fertile soil in his fist. I realized he had a bad case of "down-home back-to-your-roots" blues.

As a pastor, I've performed many funeral services, and I often do something a minister is never supposed to do. I cry. The minister is supposed to be the comforter and consoler, the rock of strength supporting the grieving family. But when I see grown sons and daughters trying to express to a corpse what they never expressed to the living being they've loved and lost, I cry. I'd conducted enough funerals where this had been the case to resolve I'd never be in a similar situation.

I approached my brothers about a plan to give our father a living memorial—now, while he was alive—in the form of a tractor. And not just any tractor, but *the* tractor. The one he'd always wanted, complete with a front-end loader and a backhoe. The whole works.

All five of us agreed. After we finished our planning and scheming, we announced a surprise birthday party for Dad. When he had opened all his presents, we told him we had one more very special gift and led him to the window. Seeing the tractor, he placed his hands over his face and cried. My brothers and I cried, too, not for the things we hadn't done but in thankfulness for being able to seize a precious opportunity to express love while it could still be received.♥

A FRUITFUL RIDE IN THE RAIN

Julianna Simon

My father is very thrifty—perhaps even compulsively so. When I was growing up, my family never once owned a major appliance that wasn't a dented floor model purchased at a discount price. Dad got them ridiculously cheap, and they usually worked all right. To this day, if Dad buys a present for any of us he leaves the "reduced for quick sale" tags on it out of sheer pride in his buying prowess.

If an item isn't on sale, he simply doesn't buy it. One of his favorite jokes plays off this theme: "Some kids get dropped at the doorstep by a stork, but we got you on blue-light special at KMart and they charge extra for delivery so we had to carry you home."

On a family vacation ten years ago, Dad talked me into a "father-daughter adventure" that entailed bicycling nine miles in a thunderstorm to buy oranges on sale for five cents less per dozen than they cost at the store around the corner. Indulging my father's quest for cheap oranges, I soon found myself riding through the pouring rain. There were huge puddles in the road, so we were practically drowned by the spray every time a car went by.

After an especially ferocious dunking, courtesy of a pickup truck that almost ran us over as well as drenching us, I howled in frustration, "Why are we doing this? This is crazy!"

Dad abruptly braked his bike (bought on sale at 60 percent off the sticker price) and turned to face me. I skidded to a stop just inches short of his rear wheel. Even with his drenched clothing and the rain dripping off his nose and chin, Dad looked dignified. "Julianna," he said, "it's really very simple. You know I grew up during the Depression. My family had to take in boarders to keep a roof over our heads and food on the table. My job was buying groceries and household goods for my mother. In my whole childhood, the only time she ever said anything nice to me was when I brought home supplies at a good sale price."

With his words, my crankiness washed away. I reached out and squeezed my father's hand. Then we both pedalled off with a clearer sense of the force behind our journey. I can't say I was exactly enthusiastic about riding all that way in the rain, but I was buoyed by a deeper sense of understanding and compassion for my father.♥

WHAT ARE YOU WILLING TO GIVE UP?

Sharon Lambert

My father will never be remembered for his financial wealth or for his education. His schooling consisted of eight years in a one-room school and one year in a business academy. He was a farmer all his working life. For over 71 years he loved and lived with the same woman he married.

In the outside world, the name "Newell Lambert" may call up no special recognition or memories. But in my private world, it stands for love and wisdom.

When I was six years old, I was diagnosed with scoliosis. I spent all my elementary and high school years wearing a cast or brace. When the cast could no longer stop the curving of my spine, surgery became necessary. The operation was "successful"—it stopped the curvature process—but it meant facing life as a hunchback. Not surprisingly, this was very hard for me to accept. But at least I no longer had to use a cast or brace.

Years later, as a college student, I was home for summer vacation when I fell off a horse and broke my collarbone. I was back in a brace again and found it easy to get into a "feel sorry for me" mood. That's the mood I was in one warm midsummer day when my father, who had been working outside, came in to see me. I was sitting in a big rocker, crying. When Dad asked what was wrong, I told him that I'd give everything—*everything*—to be like everyone else.

Dad looked at me for a long time. "Everything?" he finally asked. "Your sisters and brothers, their teasing and their love?"

"That's not what I meant," I said, as I continued crying.

"Oh, you'd give up your home and security, just to be like everyone else?"

"No," I sobbed. Didn't he understand what I was saying? Or was it I who didn't understand the full meaning of the words I had cried out to him in my frustration?

My father had bent over my chair as he talked to me. I looked straight into his eyes, and for the first time ever, I saw tears in them. He straightened up. "Everything?" he asked. "Even the love your mom and I have for you?" Then he opened the screen door and walked out.

Dad doesn't remember that event, but it changed my life. It made me aware for the first time that I'm God's special creation—that there is excitement in just being me, exactly as I am—and that the blessings of love, family, and security far outweigh any physical condition.

There have been times since when I still want to be physically like everyone else. Then I see my dad in his blue, long-sleeved cotton workshirt and his bib Key overalls and straw hat bending over me, I hear his words, and I remember a gift of love and wisdom given on a warm, summer afternoon.♥

WHO'S ON FIRST?

Rick Carson

I was waiting in the back yard with my 30-year-old Rawlings PM5 fielder's glove while my nine-year-old son, Jonah, at my suggestion, had bolted upstairs in search of the mitt I'd recently bought him.

In 1955 Lubbock, Texas, it had been a crisp, sunny day much like this one when my team, the Scrappers, had beaten the Rockets 3 to 2 in an extra-inning Little League game. We had a new field (built by the Lion's Club), new bleachers (ACE Hardware), and an official, built-to-perfection Little League specification pitcher's mound. On that special day, I'd been atop it.

I threw the ball hard that day. I pitched good. My teammates chattered, "You got him, Babe," "You're in charge, Richard," "Hey batter, hey batter," and—best of all—"You're the one, Big Rick." In one game I'd gone from plain Richard to "Big Rick." "Elated" fails to adequately capture how I felt that day.

The memory intensified my desire to "Play ball!" I wished Jonah would hurry.

Hurry up, I thought, stepping off the official Little League distance between an imaginary pitching rubber and home plate. Jonah and I could build a mound on that spot where grass hardly grew anyway. Home plate could go over there, and the fence would be a backstop. Today, though, we'd just play catch. Or maybe I'd toss the ball lightly to him, and he'd tap it back to me with the bat. It'll help Jonah learn to keep his eye on the ball, I thought. He probably won't be a home run hitter. I wasn't. But he'll be a solid, reliable hitter. And a great pitcher. Good arms run in the family. I'll help him take care of his arm. No curves for years. I threw too many. Probably why my pitching career peaked at 16. I don't like to think about it.

Where was Jonah, for goodness' sake?

I tossed myself several pop-ups, catching them Willie Mays-style. Willie was the best. I'd seen him play an exhibition game in 1956. I was 11. Willie, the incomparable and world-renowned center fielder for the Giants, had looked at me and nodded. He looked right into my eyes. I'd been too star-struck to nod back, and it's a moment I'd like to live over. This time I'd say, "Say hey, Willie. Say hey." Willie used to say "Say hey" a lot, or so I'd heard. Too bad Jonah never saw Willie play. I'd tell him about Willie Mays, but I'd emphasize the importance of learning the fundamentals of fielding before trying to catch Willie-style.

Where was Jonah?

I threw a few onto the roof and, as they rolled off, I scooped them out of the air, faking a perfect peg to home. I reminded myself to tell Jonah to keep the ball low on his pegs when playing the outfield and to remember to check where his runners were before every pitch. He'd have to watch runners as a pitcher, too, and learn to throw from a stretch.

So much to learn. We'd have to start now. I went inside and yelled. "Jonah, hurry up. Jonah, what's up, pal? Jonah?"

I ran upstairs. No Jonah. I sprinted downstairs and into the front yard, still sporting ball and glove. My wife, Leti, was repotting a plant.

"You seen Jonah?"

With a side glance, she said, "He's at Brennen's playing Nintendo."

My denial systems flew up like an armored shield. "No," I said, as if she were sorely mistaken. "He and I are going to play catch."

"All I know is, Brennen came by, Jonah asked if he could go play Nintendo, and they left."

No catch. No high flies. Nintendo? Freckle-faced Brennen chosen over the pitching ace of the Scrappers? My heart fell into my stomach.

I sluffed back through the house to the back yard. Disappointment is a feeling like no other. It wracked my guts and made my bones ache. Seconds later, a funny loneliness set in—a longing—for Jonah, for somebody to play catch with, for times past. To be "Big Rick," maybe. I thought, This is how little boys feel when their dads are too busy for them, not how dads feel when their little boys are too busy for *them*. I fielded a few more off the roof, but there was no zip in it.

Later, after supper, I told Jonah that he'd left me stranded and I was miffed. He looked at me with the wisdom of a sage, put his hand on my shoulder, and said—I swear—precisely these words: "Dad, I love you and I like you and we have the rest of our lives together. Don't worry about it."

It was exactly what I needed to hear. I felt soothed, yet off balance. Who was the older, wiser one here, anyway? There must have been a typo and Opie had gotten Andy's lines.

It's been that way with Jonah and me a few times since because, drat it, there is no script. He's never been my son before, nor I his dad. This puts us in the position of figuring things out as we go along. It's not a bad deal. In fact, all in all, I like it. While life experience is valuable, there's something to be said for a fresh point of view. There's an essence to who we really are. It's had many labels: "soul" for one.

There are many wise souls on our planet. And it's possible that some of them are housed in small bodies, love Nintendo, and have never heard of Willie Mays.♥

BUTTERFLY STONES

Dave Cowles

Vacations—even those that seem the most ordinary—can be the greatest times in a kid's life. One of those times occurred for me the summer my parents rented a cottage, sight unseen, in the little town of Marysville on Lake Huron.

I was 9 that summer. My brother was 11, and my sister was 5. The cottage was on a bluff overlooking the lake. Water and kids seem to have a natural affinity for one another, so after unpacking our gear we immediately charged down the steps to check out the "beach." It turned out to be more hard-packed clay than sand, and when we tried to wade into the water, we found our tender feet negotiating a bed of rocks.

Hearing sounds of agony and disappointment from us kids, Dad made his way down the steps to investigate. While he assured us that things weren't as bad as they looked, he had trouble hiding his own negative appraisal of the situation. It was clearly a vacation disaster in the making.

As he stepped to the edge of the water and

looked down at the treacherous stones beneath the breaking waves, his eye caught something in the surf. Bending down, he reached into the froth and pulled out a small, shiny, worn, almost geometric-shaped stone.

"Hey, you monkeys, look at this!" he called out.

We ran to where he was standing in the water, and he held out his treasure for us to see. He said it was a fossil of a critter from the age of the dinosaurs. He called it a "butterfly stone."

Looking closer, we saw a tiny miracle. The fossil was only an inch or so wide and looked for all the world like a small butterfly with its wings extended. Dad, a veteran of years of Boy Scouting, had a trained eye for such things. He explained to us that butterfly stones are really the leftover skeletons of something called "brachiopods."

He looked at our "beach" and decided it was worth another scan to see if there were more fossils around.

The four of us walked about a quarter of a mile along the water's edge, eyes pinned to the ground. In ten minutes we had found three more.

All disappointment left, thoughts of swimming and sand castles faded, and a brand new adventure captured our imaginations. For the next week we walked the water's edge with Dad, collecting fossils, and before our vacation ended we had harvested 60 or 70 butterfly stones. I still have several. Every time I look at them I'm reminded of the summer Dad showed us how to make the best of a bad situation and taught us the pleasures and rewards of beachcombing.

Ordinary times. Extraordinary memories.♥

THANK YOU, DAD;
THANK YOU, DAUGHTER

Joachim de Posada

We all face tough times in life. Some of us have it tougher than others. But everyone, without exception, will go through bad times.

Certainly, I'm no exception. I recall one of those bad times in my life and how the bond my dad had created between us got me through it. It happened when I was 12 years old.

On January 1, 1959, a man named Fidel Castro assumed power by force of a little island country named Cuba. He promised a future of democracy and free elections to a country that really needed it. But my father didn't believe what most Cubans did, and from the first day of Castro's regime, Dad warned that we would all be fooled by this charismatic young leader.

Several days after the takeover, my grandmother, my best friend, Tito, and I went to Walgreens, where Tito saw some revolution caps. He wanted me to ask my grandmother to buy one for each of us. Although I knew how my father felt about Castro, I asked. My grandmother was reluctant, but she agreed to buy the caps.

When my father came home for lunch that day, he saw me wearing the cap. He was very angry. Calling me to him, he said, "If I ever see you with that communist cap on again, I'll tear your head off." This was an extreme comment for my father, who never laid a finger on me in anger.

"I'm sorry, Dad," I said, and I took the cap off and put it in the back pocket of my pants.

That afternoon I went to play with my friend Tito at his house. Tito was the son of the Argentinian ambassador to Cuba. A party was being held for Castro in the Argentine embassy that evening, recognizing him as the new ruler of Cuba. Tito asked his father if he and I could attend the party. We were told absolutely not; it was for adults only. But Tito was insistent and managed to get permission for us to go if we agreed to stay in the kitchen and away from where the party was being held. We agreed.

Standing on a table in the kitchen and looking through a window, Tito and I found we could see the party in progress. All the important people were there: the American ambassador, many government officials, Ambassador Porfirio Rubirosa, who was very famous at the time and who occasionally gave us advice on how to be charming to ladies. I could even see my parents through the window.

Suddenly there were people rushing toward the front door of the embassy. I saw Castro himself coming inside with a group of bodyguards. He didn't say hello to anyone; he simply walked across the room, asked where the kitchen was, and came inside, where he began to greet the cooks, servants, and waiters. Then he spotted us, a couple of young teenagers. When I told him who I was, he said he knew my father. Then Tito introduced himself as the ambassador's son.

Castro suggested that we all take a picture together. When I turned around, he saw the revolution cap in my pocket and asked me to put it on for the photograph. I said no, but he kept asking me to put it on. And I kept saying no. I took it out of my pocket and showed it to him, but I wouldn't put it on.

By this time many people were coming into the kitchen. Photographers were pointing their cameras at us, and here was this kid saying "no" to the most powerful man in the country— something no one had dared to do before. Things were getting tense, and I was getting worried.

I looked to the kitchen door, where people were still coming in, and suddenly I spotted my father. He was signaling with his hand toward his head, his lips mouthing, *Put the cap on.* And I did—because my father said it was okay.

My dad earned my loyalty and respect over the years to the point where no one, even the most powerful man in Cuba, could make me do something he had told me not to do. He was my hero. He gave me the strength to face adversity in life, and I've tried, in parenting my own daughter, to pass on his legacy.

One day, when my daughter was 13 years old, about the same age I was when I chose to obey Dad instead of Castro, she wrote me the following letter.

Dear Dad,

Hi, how are you? I am very happy, that is why I am writing this letter. You must be wondering—"Why is she writing this letter?" Well, I'm going to answer you. The reason I'm writing this letter is because I want to say Thank You.

A few days ago I turned 13. Can you believe it? I'm already a teenager! Well, throughout these 13 years you have not only been the most understanding, loving, let's not forget "unique," father in the world. You have been the best friend I could ever have. You were there for me when I had problems. You were there for me when I didn't feel like the greatest nor smartest person in the world. You were there when I was so afraid of going to a psychologist, you were there in 6th grade when I got really sick and lost 20 pounds, and you have been here this year when I haven't been getting along with my mom or getting the best of grades, and most important we were there for each other when we both lost something that we truly loved, my sister.

Because of problems I have faced in my life I have grown up faster than I should, but I could have never faced these problems, no matter how grown up I was, without you. I have grown up a very happy child because of the love that you have given me.

They say that being a teenager will be the happiest time of your life. That is true but it is also confusing. There have been many times when I have felt confused, sad or lonely, and the only thing that got me going was that little phone call I made to my dad. You always have a way of making me feel good, or at least better.

You have also given me something I really need, trust. It may not seem the most important thing, but it is very important to me. You have been one of the only people who has trusted me. In fact you have been the person that has trusted me the most and, believe it or not, when I have to make a decision to do bad or good I do good only because I wouldn't betray that trust for the world. Your trust has given me self-respect, pride, dignity, and has made me the girl I am today.

Another thing is that I feel we have a special bond, in which I can talk to you openly about anything without a doubt in my mind that even if you don't agree with me you will help me and understand me without blowing up.

Now I have a boyfriend, Albert, and I like him a lot (even though he is short) and I hope you do too. I want you to know that until the day I die, you will be my favorite guy in the world, and if I have surpassed your every expectation of a daughter it is only because you have surpassed my every expectation as a father, a teacher, and a friend. Like every other person you have your faults, but in my eyes God created a masterpiece.

Thank you for being the light at the end of the tunnel, and even though you accept the fact that I am growing up, and you are treating me in that way, I want you to know I will ALWAYS be your little girl.

Love always and forever,
Your daughter
Caroline Marie♥

THE LAST GAME

Kenneth G. Davis

I knew this would be our last trip to the ballpark together, and my memories were illuminated like Wrigley Field beneath its newly added lights. For years, Dad and I had celebrated the arrival of each new spring by making our ritual pilgrimage to the Cubs' home opener. We took the "el" from our bluecollar neighborhood of Rogers Park across town to Waveland Avenue, and a short walk later we would enter the mystical green cathedral known as the "friendly confines." We shared our communion of hot dogs and sodas as we watched the teams go through their pregame drills. Dad always said that if you don't get there in time for batting practice, it doesn't count as a real game.

Dad had endured many trials and tribulations living through the Depression, World War II, and the Korean War, but none was as painful as the agony of being a diehard Cubs fan. He suffered through countless losing seasons, but he never lost his devotion to the perpetually hapless

Cubbies and never lost his sense of humor either. He reminded us on numerous occasions that the Cubs changed managers more often than Italy changed presidents. One of his favorite quotes came from a recent Cub manager who, when queried about the fact that the team hadn't won a pennant since 1945, said, "Well, any team can have a bad century."

And the Cubs did. But, through endless losing seasons, Dad kept his sense of humor and his perspective. I recall with vivid detail his deep, soulful laugh when, after a game marked by unsurpassed ineptness, the manager was asked in a postgame interview what he thought about his team's execution and replied, "I'm in favor of it."

The more the Cubs lost, the more Dad loved them. His affection transcended the team's performance, and he recognized that their foibles and ineptitudes could serve as a textbook for teaching a young child the meaning of sacrifice, teamwork, anticipation, and patience. (As in, "Wait till next year.")

After I moved away to Houston, I thought about those lessons a lot. I tried to get back to Chicago at least once a year during the season, and Dad and I haven't missed but one or two years in the past 20. Unfortunately, one was the year they made the playoffs.

After I received the phone call, I knew I had to make one more trip to Chicago and one last trip to Wrigley with Dad.

I carried him aboard the el, and we headed toward Waveland Avenue in a reversal of roles that had begun four decades earlier. We arrived a couple of hours before game time. Batting practice had not even started, although a few of the Houston players were playing catch in the outfield. We made our way through the left-field bleachers down to the brick wall covered with a brown, lifeless tangle that later in the season would green into Wrigley Field's renowned ivy.

Two of the visiting Houston outfielders were loosening up and playing catch, and one of them came over to retrieve an errant ball. He looked up at me just as I was spreading Dad's ashes onto the sacred turf. Shaking his head in disbelief, he trotted away to rejoin his teammates.

Having completed my mission and fulfilled Dad's last request, I was escorted out of Wrigley Field by a rotund security guard.

Sweet dreams, Dad.♥

POPS AND THE FOUNTAIN OF YOUTH

Sidney B. Simon

My father is 88 years old. He lives in a condo in Ft. Lauderdale. His life isn't glorious. He goes fishing once a month, plays cards once a week, and takes naps daily. In between, he watches a lot of TV.

I was worried about him, and it occurred to me that maybe I should try to get him interested in a computer. His mind is still sharp, and I remember that he used to type when I was a boy. He would make up stories to tell my brother and me. Some of them were darn good, so we asked him to tell them over and over. When he got bored, he'd type them up and make us read them.

I phoned him. He'd been napping in front of the TV. I could hear it in the background.

"Hi, Pop. How you doin'?"

"How could I be doing? I just missed my soap opera," he said.

"Ah, Pop. I'm sorry."

"Don't feel bad. I taped it."

"You tape your soap operas?" I must have sounded incredulous.

"You think I wanna be trapped in this stinking condo every day just to see a soap opera?" he said. "I watch 'em when it's convenient. Sometimes even out of cycle. Doesn't matter. I can always predict who's going to die and who's going to get pregnant."

It was a perfect lead. "That's funny, Pop. I've been thinking about you and the stories you used to tell us when we were kids. Remember? You were a great storyteller, and we could never predict how your stories would come out. You always fooled us."

"Yeah, I was pretty good. I liked telling you kids stories. You were always appreciative. You'd coax and coax. Finally I got fed up and typed them out and told you to go read 'em yourself."

"I remember, Pop. Whatever happened to those stories? I'd love to see them again."

He waited a long time before he answered. "They went with your mother. I don't know where she stored them. When she died, I just threw things out. All kinds of things. I had to do that. Ghosts were everywhere." His voice faltered a bit. "I never wrote about ghosts. Didn't know how to handle them."

"I know, Pop. I know." I couldn't think of anything else to say to him. It had been ten years, but the grief still overcame him. My brother and I were careful not to mention Mom much. It could sink him for days.

I tried to lighten my voice. "Hey, Pop, I've got a great idea. I think you should try to recapture some of those stories. We've got an extra computer at the office. Next time I come to visit I'm going to bring it down for you."

"She kept my stories in a brown cardboard box. She loved my stories. She was so proud when I typed them up for you kids." That was his only reply.

When I phoned him after that, he never mentioned any interest in the computer or in rewriting the stories. But I was determined. In fact, it became an obsession. So when it came time for my annual visit, I packed up the XT with the small green monitor that nobody at the office was using. I bought a little dot matrix printer that I found on sale, bubble-packed the equipment into three boxes, checked them as baggage at the airline counter, and hoped for smooth landings.

When the plane arrived in Ft. Lauderdale, I was surprised to find my father waiting at the luggage carousel. Usually I caught a cab to the condo.

"Surprise, Big Shot," he greeted me. "I got us a limousine. Figured that if I'm getting a computer to become a famous writer, a limousine was a cheap investment. I almost called the media." He laughed at his own cleverness, and I could feel his belly shake when I hugged him. "I didn't acknowledge your computer idea because I was too excited, and I wanted my limousine pickup to be a real surprise for you."

I hugged him again, and he kept belly shaking. He was so tickled with himself.

The three computer boxes were there, seemingly unharmed. I mounted them on my trusty wheels, and we rolled them out to the limo. Pop was in charge. He gave the driver directions, and we both settled back into the luxurious cushions, joking and laughing all the way to the condo, glad to be together. Pop gave the driver a nice tip.

We rode the elevator up to his apartment. It sparkled. Pop always keeps his things clean and orderly. Although I thought I'd take him out for dinner, the table was already set. "You'll notice we're eating in," he said. "I barbecued a chicken— me and the deli—and I made a salad and tapioca pudding—also with a little help from the deli. So we're all set. Anyway," he added, "I want to learn the computer."

I wasn't about to argue with him. Together we unpacked the boxes. I borrowed a small screw driver and screwed in the monitor and the printer cables. He watched closely. I could see he would know how to do it next time. He was like that.

I showed him the printer cable and the tapered shape of the metal shell. "Only goes one way?" he asked. I nodded.

I had put the software he'd need on the machine, and before I left home I'd written him a little database for his addresses and phone numbers. I put in all his grandkids and the few relatives he hadn't outlived. I knew he'd be impressed. I guess you never outgrow your need to impress your old man.

"Okay, Mr. Computerman, boot it up and let's see what you got," he said, after I'd completed the setup.

I looked at him with surprise. "Pop, where'd you learn to say that?"

"You think you're the only one who knows computer? I got a friend. Of course, he's got a 386, but he promised not to look down his nose at me with my XT."

I hugged him, and that belly just kept shaking with laughter.

So I booted it up and showed him how to load the word processing program and start typing.

"Which key saves what I write?" he asked. I told him.

"And when I want it back?" I showed him that, and how to save his files in some order. I recommended .ltr for letters, .str for stories, and .pas for passionate love letters. He laughed.

"So—I'm going to write. Let me be now, okay?"

I kissed him on the top of his head and said, "Go to it, Hemingway."

An hour later he came out of the computer room, and he looked five years younger. It was shocking. Five years. Creases that had etched his face were gone. Bags under his tired eyes had vanished. It was really eerie. I was speechless.

"I'm ready to print. Come show me how to print what I've written."

All I could say was, "Dad, you look great. You look, somehow . . . You look . . . "

He finished my sentence. "Younger. I've found the fountain of youth. It's called 'computer.' Now, come show me how to print."

I wrote the printing commands out for him on a 3x5 card. He caught on right away. He was a natural. So I showed him how to number pages, and we wrote that down on a 3x5 card, too. The printer started to chatter and he shooed me away.

I went out onto the screened porch and started reading one of the books I'd brought. It was a novel, and it caught my interest. I was into Chapter Three when Pop emerged. *My God!* I thought. *His silver hair has gone black!*

"So, don't look so shocked. I finished my story. Here it is. You remember 'The Freckled Knight'?"

"Oh, Pops," I said. "You rewrote 'The Freckled Knight'?"

"It was easy. I like this word processor thing. It makes the typewriter seem primitive. And I remembered why I wrote the story in the first place. What was it—60 years ago?"

"More like 55, Pop. I was in the first grade."

"And some bully kid was picking on you because you had freckles. And you hated them. You wanted me to rub them off or get something from your mother to cover them up with."

I went to him and put my arms around him. "You were so good, Pops. You made up this story to make me appreciate my freckles. And you know what? I've loved them ever since. Because of you."

"Not because of me. They come from your mother's side. The whole family was a bunch of freckled knights," he said.

"You know what I mean. Because of you I came to love my freckles. Because of you."

He raised his hands as if to keep things from getting too sentimental. "So here's the story. I still need a little help figuring out when you use backspace and when to use delete, so it's not perfect. But it's not bad for the first time out on a computer, huh?"

I looked at the page, turning it into the light. "Not bad, not bad at all for a 70-year-old."

He grinned. I don't think he'd seen his black

hair yet. Nor had he gotten a view of a face with missing wrinkles. But he grinned anyhow. "Gotta get back to my computer. I want to get down another one I told you boys."

"Which one, Pop? Which one?" I asked excitedly.

As he'd done so often when we were young, he said, "Hold your pants on. Don't you like a little surprise?"

"Sure, Pops. But you're in for one yourself," I said.

"What do you mean?"

"You'll see. You're not the only one who knows how to set up a surprise. You just wait."

He went back to the computer, and for another hour he banged away at the keyboard. I read "The Freckled Knight" and my eyes welled with tears. He had recaptured it with all of its tender nuances. When my eyes dried, I read some more of my novel, and then I heard the printer singing. He came out trailing another printout. And, believe it or not, he was another ten years younger. I saw it first in his smile. It revealed not his 88-year-old choppers but the big buck teeth I remembered from when we were kids and he was young. And the folds at his neck were gone.

"So, how did you like 'The Freckled Knight,' my bucko?" he asked. "If you liked that, wait till you read my newest version of 'Sparky the Firefly.' You remember Sparky, I hope?" He was flashing that bucktoothed grin from ear to ear.

"Pops, this is a miracle," I said.

"A miracle that I should remember these stories?" I knew he hadn't looked into the mirror yet.

"Yes, that's it, Pops. That's it."

He turned to go back into the computer room. "I want to get one more done before I take my nap. It's burning in me. It'll be a piece of cake to get it out."

"Which one, Pop?"

"Hold your pants on. You'll see. Just wait. Get a little patience. You want to grow up without the capacity to wait?"

"Not me, Pops. I can wait. You go get 'em. It's not easy, but I know I can wait. In the meantime, I'll read 'Sparky.' 'The Freckled Knight' made me cry."

"You're talking to an accomplished writer," he said. "Now also a professional computer word processor. You ain't seen nothin' yet." He turned and went back to his computer. I could hear the keys lightly clicking, faster and crisper. I imagined the story lighting up his little green screen. And I pictured his young face glowing in the green light.

About a half-hour later, he came out. "The printer won't print. I heard a little bell sound, and now the printer won't print." He looked exactly the way he used to look when I was a first grader. Exactly. My face must have gone ghostly white. My mouth hung open. Pop looked at me and became agitated. "What's the matter? Did I break the computer? Did I do something wrong? Can it be fixed?"

"No, Pops. Nothing with the computer. Well, maybe it has to do with the computer. But the printer's not broken. You've just been writing up such a storm you used up all the paper I'd put in it. That bell was the printer telling you you're out of paper. I can fix it in a jiffy."

"Oh. Your face made me think I'd broken an expensive computer for good. Don't scare me like that. My heart can't take it." And he laughed.

I kept staring at him. He was so young.

We went back into the computer room. I showed him how to load the continuous feed paper, and when he entered the print command it chattered along happily. He forgot I was there. He was busy reading the new story as it came off the printer. I looked over his shoulder. This is what he had written.

The Fountain of Youth

by Frank Simon

I have found the fountain of youth. It has 104 keys. I counted them. I have learned to use most of them. I stay away from the key that says "END." It's the one I fear the most.

The fountain of youth is available to any older person. If your son gives you a computer, it's the best way to get one. If you have stories to write, the fountain of youth works most miraculously.

I know, because I found it. And, yes, my son, I looked in the mirror. It works. It is true. I am just the way you remembered me when you were a little kid. If you sit in my lap, I will read "The Freckled Knight" to you.

The printer said more. After all, it was his story. But I put my arms around his waist, and I held him tight. Then I picked him up—his frail bones weighed so little—and I carried him to the couch and sat with him in my lap, and read to him out loud. First, "The Freckled Knight," then "Sparky the Firefly," and we cried together.

The next day his hair got gray again. The choppers returned, and so did the wrinkles. I guess when you're 88 you can't stay forever young.

But I'll tell you something. You can believe it or not, but every time he goes into that computer room and works on one of his old stories for us old kids of his, he comes out looking 10, or 20, or 30 years younger. So what if those buck teeth I love are only temporary?

What I pray for now is that he postpones as long as possible using that "END" key.♥

III.

MOTHERS

FIRST DAY OF SCHOOL

Ann Brewster

Every day she would hear the kids across the street playing in the school yard. How she wanted to be over there having fun, too. "Can't I go over there and play, Mother?" she'd plead.

"No, not now," her mother would explain. "Those kids have work to do, and you might bother them."

"But when can I go to school?" she'd ask.

"When you're five," her mother said.

So she rode her bike, the one with three wheels, up and down the sidewalk in front of her house. She rang the bell on the handlebar just to hear the merry sound. She couldn't wait till she was five.

The day finally came: the first day of school. She wore a pretty dress and sat patiently while her mother brushed each blond curl around her finger and put a bow in her hair. Then, holding hands, they walked across the street and up to the school. Up the front steps to the door. Up the inside steps to the kindergarten room.

This was a special day; the day she had dreamed of for so long.

"Will you be okay, Ann?" her mother asked, a little anxiously.

"Yes, Mother," her daughter replied, then added, "Remember, I have work to do, so please don't come over and bother me, okay?"

Her mother gave her a little hug and turned to go, but not before Ann noticed a tear on her cheek. Why would her mother cry on such a wonderful day? she wondered.♥

SOMEBODY

Chick Moorman

Somebody's mother baked chocolate chip cookies. Four dozen. The familiar aroma of fresh treats tantalized her seven- and nine-year-old sons. Equally tempting was the sight of melting chunks of chocolate peeking out of warm, golden brown, freshly baked dough. Cooling on the kitchen table within sight, smell, touch, and taste, the cookies commanded attention.

Somebody's mother announced to both boys the cookies were for eating. After dinner. The cookies were dessert, to be rationed throughout the week.

When his mother went out to run an errand, somebody decided to get a close-up view of the cookies. Visual stimulation was not off limits, and chocolate chip cookies are certainly attractive. No harm in looking.

Somebody found close proximity to the cookies intoxicating and decided one corner of one cookie couldn't possibly be missed. So somebody helped himself to a single chunk, making sure the pilfered piece contained several of the coveted chips.

After teasing his senses with a portion of a cookie, somebody realized how obvious it was that a piece was missing. So somebody destroyed the evidence by depositing it in his stomach. Somebody then rearranged the remaining cookies to obscure the vacancy.

Believe it or not, somebody enjoyed eating that cookie so much, his rational mind set out to get him another one. One more cookie wouldn't be missed, somebody's mind reasoned. So somebody ate chocolate chip cookie number two and again adjusted the cookies to conceal the larceny.

If chocolate chip cookies are tasty, are stolen chocolate chip cookies even tastier? They were to somebody. So he ate a third one and continued the ritual of rearranging the remaining cookies.

Somebody's brain must have been affected by the chocolate because he kept eating cookies and rearranging them until over a dozen had disappeared. At that point, somebody figured that some other body might notice if he continued to eat cookies. Besides, somebody was full. So he stopped.

Later, somebody's mother called both boys into the kitchen and demanded to know what had happened to the cookies.

"I don't know," said the seven-year-old.

"Neither do I," said the nine-year-old.

"Somebody's lying," said the mother, not knowing who "somebody" was.

After a series of failed bribes, threats, and lectures, somebody was sent to his room. So was his brother. "You two can come out as soon as somebody confesses," said the mother. Nobody did.

Somebody went to his brother and proposed that they take the blame together. Somebody's innocent sibling declined. Somebody's father entered the equation and applied equally humane but ineffective parenting techniques. Still, somebody held tightly to his secret and refused to confess.

The frustrated parents found no strategy to get somebody to tell the truth and eventually the boys were released from their bondage without an adequate explanation of what had happened to the cookies.

As the years passed, the chocolate chip cookie caper became the family joke. It was often alluded to during 40 years of family gatherings. During those four decades, both somebody and his brother maintained their innocence.

The time came when somebody's mother was diagnosed with a terminal illness. She had baked a lot of chocolate chip cookies during her 75 years, and during that time it had seemed as though her cookie-making days would never end. But that had been an illusion. Somebody's mother began to move slowly and only with the aid of a walker or a cane. Soon she was confined to bed. When she could no longer speak, she wrote. When she could no longer write, the family gathered once more to help ease her transition into the next world.

At a time when no one else was around, somebody snuck into his mother's room and lay next to her in bed. He held her hand and stroked it softly. He talked to her in whispers about their life together. He told her he loved her, and she nodded. He shared his recognition and appreciation of her love. She nodded again.

"Can you keep a secret?" he asked. Another nod. "You won't tell anybody?" She shook her head sideways.

After glancing around to be sure no one was listening, somebody shared a secret with his mother, whispering in her ear everything he knew about chocolate chip cookies. Somebody's mother smiled, and they shared a final hug.♥

A WOMAN OF THE '90s

Diane Hodges

In many ways, my mother was a typical mom. She knew nothing, and I knew everything. How could anyone live so long and know so little? After all, don't you know all there is to know about *everything* in the first 14 years of life?

My mother was beautiful. Actually, she was gorgeous. She was also bright, articulate, creative, and personable, but she never knew it. She would have made a successful businesswoman, but she was ahead of her time. Her "career" was raising children and following my dad around the world.

She and I didn't often agree on much. We sparred my whole childhood. To say we were "dysfunctional" is an understatement. The one thing she could count on me to do was the exact opposite of anything she valued or thought was best for me.

- She thought I should major in home ec. I majored in communications (definitely a degree you can starve to death with).

- She thought I should get married. I got a master's degree.
- She still thought I should get married. I got a Ph.D. (She told me if I wanted a doctorate to marry one.)
- She told me I should spend money on a car. I spent it climbing mountains with Outward Bound.
- She thought I should get a job in our hometown. I took a job in New York City.
- She kept people at a distance. I hug everyone.
- She talked about having plastic surgery (but couldn't spend money on herself). I had it.
- She talked of trips she'd never take. I took them.
- She kept out of the spotlight. I became a speaker.

How could two people be such opposites? Why was she so conservative, and why was I so rebellious? How many times I wished we could have an amicable mother/daughter relationship, but it was clearly not to be.

As my mother aged, she became frail and ill, and my visits to Florida became more frequent. One night I walked into her kitchen. The lights were off, but the streetlights silhouetted her face. I could see tears trickling down her cheeks. I asked why she was crying. She responded, "I'm not crying because I'm going to die. I'm crying because I never lived."

I couldn't believe what I was hearing. Hadn't she tried endlessly to try to make me like her—to live like her? It was then I realized what a gift she had given me. She prepared me to be a woman of the '90s. She taught me to be determined, to live my dreams, to have the courage to risk. She helped me develop self-confidence.

Could it be that we weren't dysfunctional after all? Perhaps she knew what she was doing all along. Perhaps she was a great teacher, for only she knew how to get me to learn and do the things in my life that she didn't do in hers.

Recently I was driving home from work with my teenage son. Engaged in casual conversation, I asked him a question. He prefaced his response with, "If you knew anything about anything, you would know . . . ."

I smiled to myself. A man of the 21st Century is under development.♥

LOVE WILL ALWAYS BRING US HOME

D. Trinidad Hunt

Lovell Harris was raised in St. Louis, Missouri, in the St. Louis Projects—one square mile of high-rise tenements housing 10,000 people. Lovell had two models: his mom and grandmother, both of whom worked overtime to support Lovell, his four brothers, and his dad, who was an abusive alcoholic.

During his early years, Lovell followed in the footsteps of his father. By the age of 18, he was drinking, and by 27 he was arrested for pushing drugs. In 1973, Lovell was incarcerated. The day he went to prison he was so sick from alcohol abuse that he was urinating blood.

While he was in prison, Lovell began to dry out. He started visiting the prison library and read his first book, *Treasure Island*, from cover to cover.

At the same time, Lovell was beginning to have flashbacks. Without alcohol and drugs to dull his senses, memories of his youth began to surface. He saw his grandmother's face and her beautiful, wrinkled old hands as she knelt before him to wrap his feet in rags to protect them from the bitter winter cold. Collected from the garbage dumps, these rags were washed and hung out to dry, then saved as a replacement for socks for her five grandsons who had to walk to school every day.

He saw his mother's face as she watched him walk out into the night after stealing money from her purse to buy drugs. He felt her heartbreak, and he heard her words echoing in his ears. "Lovell, you're a special boy. Someday you're going to be all right, son. Someday you're going to make your mother proud."

About seven months passed behind those prison walls, and Lovell continued to think of his mother and of her belief in him. Then one day a rumor spread; there was going to be a rumble. The men were planning a breakout.

On the day of the jailbreak, Lovell stayed in his cell. When his best friend came to get him, he was sitting on his bunk staring straight ahead at the wall.

"Come on, Lovell," his friend yelled. "This is it!"

"I'm not going, man." Lovell sat frozen in position, his fingers dug into the mattress, his eyes focused straight ahead.

"Come on, Lovell!" his friend screamed.

"No, man. I'm not going."

"Don't be a wimp, Lovell," his prison mate shouted at him. "Come on!"

"I said I'm not going, man," Lovell repeated,

still staring straight ahead.

The riot that day turned out to be the worst in the history of the St. Louis, Missouri, Penitentiary. It went on for hours and dozens of men were hurt, but Lovell did not participate in any of it. It was the first time in ten years that Lovell said no. Over the years he had said yes to alcohol and yes to taking and selling drugs. This was the first time he'd stood his ground and just said *no*.

Because of that singular stand, Lovell was called before the parole board earlier than expected. He received his parole for good behavior after nine months of incarceration.

Lovell stayed clean after that. He joined the United States Navy and slowly began to build a healthy record of service to our nation. He had a lot of things to work through—much anger, hurt and pain had to be released—but over the years he steadily improved. Eventually he became a drug and alcohol abuse counselor for the Navy and was able to use his past experience to help others.

In 1987, some 15 years after he joined the Navy, Lovell was named Sailor of the Year. In 1989, he received the same award, the only person in the Navy to be given the award twice. In 1990, he received the Medal of Honor in Washington for being the number one alcohol and drug abuse counselor in the United States Navy. Lovell went on to join the reserves, and in 1993 he received the Sailor of the Year award for the Navy Reserves in the state of Hawaii.

Lovell has become all that his mother ever said he would be. He told me later that it was the images of his mother's face and the wrinkled old hands of his grandmother that kept him steady on that fateful day in prison. It was also his mother's love and her belief in him that carried him through those challenging first years outside prison walls. "Love is a saving grace," he said, "and the love of my mother finally brought me home."

Lovell Harris is one of my dearest friends. Hearing his story reminded me of my own mother and of how her belief in me carried me through so many youthful storms until I, too, was able to ride the sea of life on my own. I share Lovell's story to remind all the mothers of the world of the difference their unconditional love makes in the lives of their children.♥

EULOGY FOR MAMA

Mary Montle Bacon

"I'll kill you before the cops do!" "Don't you look at me in that tone of voice!" "I'll beat the black offa you!" "If I come back to this kitchen again and those dishes ain't washed, you'd better not be here and you'd better not be gone!"

And they say that African-American children can't do abstract reasoning!

She ruled her small family with an iron hand and a presence that seemed to follow us wherever we went, particularly in those times when we contemplated—or committed—forbidden acts. In 1995, my mama could have been reported to 911 many times for some of the things she did to us. But, even then, we knew—even if we did not like it—that it was often the fear of her wrath that kept us on the straight and narrow rather than a well-developed sense of morality or self-discipline. Even then, at a deeper level, we knew, as most children do, the difference between child rearing and child abuse, even if it felt the same.

I remember those times when we would meet
the Goodwill truck as the new delivery came in
on Monday morning—how she and my brother
and I would laugh hysterically as we tackled the
bags, tugging free what appeared to be the best of
the goodies—the clothes that would be our
Sunday best next week—washed, starched, and
crisply pressed, never embarrassing because no
one would ever suspect that they did not come off
the rack of the most stylish stores. I can still recall
the magic she performed in the kitchen as we
dined on scrambled eggs and rice or red beans
with "fatback" and rice—dishes so delicately
spiced they made us forget that we weren't
vegetarians, that the money for meat could never
quite stretch to the end of the month.

I can still see her stern expression as she
monitored the completion of homework she
couldn't possibly understand—still feel the
suppressed outrage that could never be spoken as
she insisted that it be rewritten because "no greasy
paper done at the dinner table will represent my
family in that school!" But, we did it over . . .

Even today I can still remember the
resentment welling up inside me those many
times when we had to move over in the cramped
quarters where we lived because she always
believed there was still space to take in yet
another flock of "OPKs" (other people's kids), the
ones we called "strays" who came and went with
the fluctuations of their parents' fortunes. It was
hard back then to understand the gift that she was,
why the OPKs always thought we were lucky—
actually envied us—even as we protested about
how "abused" we were.

They could see and admire that generous lady who took them in, that imposing, even overbearing, woman who impressed them with her tenaciousness, her strength, her courage as she faced life's challenges head on. It took longer for her children to understand—to see the person that she was with the clarity of their vision—for we were the ones in whom she invested her dreams, those who bore the burden of achieving the greatness only she could see as possible for us.

But, oddly enough, we knew even then that it was about love. Even then, about that, there was never a doubt. I often tell people that I had a Ph.D. long before I went to Stanford University—one that I earned over a much longer and incredibly more memorable journey from a mother with a second-grade education in the projects of the South, a mother who taught us how to "make a way out of no way."

It has been almost 25 years since she's been gone, and there are still those times when I want to say—wonder if she can hear me say—"Mama, I wish you could see me now. I wish you could know how much of you I have become . . . ."♥

LOGOPHILIA

Ben Burton

Mother wanted to speak well, worked at it, and was correct most of the time. However, she was uneasy with some words, particularly around certain people like my Uncle Anson who, when he listened—which was rarely—listened aggressively. He would examine and probe what you were saying, as you said it, and even correct your pronunciation, as you pronounced it. Mother was uneasy and unsure around him and would always plan and rehearse the things she might get to say or have to say around Uncle Anson.

While in college, I had an emergency appendectomy. Mother visited me in the hospital. On her return trip home, it was convenient for her to route back by way of Uncle Anson's. She knew he would ask about the surgery, so she began intensive preparation. She rehearsed and rehearsed *"a-pend-dec'-to-my, a-pend-dec'-to-my, a-pend-dec'-to-my,"* in order to be ready for the inquisition. The question came early, as Mother knew it would. She was nervous but practiced and ready for a fast answer.

"Well, Evalee, what kind of surgery did you say Ben had?"

A *hysterectomy*," my over-anxious mother fired back. Uncle Anson was not amused. Mother let it go as a joke anyway and proudly told us later that at least she pronounced hysterectomy correctly—"before a tough audience too!"♥

WEDDING DAY ADVICE

MaryAnn Faubion Kohl

Every young girl dreams of her wedding day. I was no exception. My "dream come true" occurred in 1968, when I was 21.

In the church foyer, my mother straightened my bridal veil and gazed into my eyes. I saw such clear love there. And something else, too. I was too young at the time to see it was the reflection of her own dreams.

I hoped she would offer me a treasure—a diamond of advice from her own rich experience I could take with me as I began my new life with my young, adoring husband. Gently she cupped my chin in her hands. I waited.

"Baby," my mother said, "never do anything around the house that you don't want to do for a lifetime, because once you start, it will be your job forever."

This was it?

"Mom," I said, "is this all you have to say to me here—now—on the brink of my new life? Is this my 'wedding day advice'?"

"Well, Baby," she said, "it's very important."

My husband and I have been happily married for 27 years now. And I think of my mother's wedding day advice every time I rev up the lawn mower.♥

MOTHER'S TABERNACLE CHOIR

Ben Burton

Many things bind families together: work, play, meals, laughter, grief, remembering, listening, talking, and celebrating. One other thing stands out on my list—singing.

Mother must have listed singing, too. It sure worked for our family. She about insisted that at least once a week—almost every Sunday night— we all get together around the piano and sing.

Everybody joined in and got to know the songs and each other better and better. When you are trying to harmonize in a small group, you get to know each other especially well. They need you and you need them. Otherwise, you're just left hanging out there on a long note with no one to cover your flaws. Families don't let that happen to each other.

The Mormon Tabernacle Choir is a great one. However, every time I hear them do one of those stirring numbers for which they are famous, I always think, Fine, but I'll bet you're not singing that number in the key of C.

They couldn't have made it in Mother's choir. In Mother's family choir we did everything in the key of C. That was the only key Mother could chord the piano in. We did the same songs over and over again each session, limited to the number of songs we could do in C.

These sessions were an intimate ritual, mainly for immediate family. Nevertheless, we couldn't be rude to near-flesh and blood. Burmadean Crump, our second or third cousin who lived over on the old Talley place about two miles away if you took the trail, crashed the group often.

And could she sing? In a word, "occasionally." Burmadean either choked up around us or just couldn't manage the key of C. Whatever the reason—even allowing for family bias— Burmadean was awful. It was so embarrassing when our dogs under the house started howling the moment Burmadean joined in. We would have to make up a quick coon story to help her save face.

But Burmadean could sing one song well and was famous for it. I mean good enough to sing it out in public—the lovely "Embraceable You." She sang it all over the county. Once Burmadean even did "Embraceable You" for a funeral. "Altered a few of the words," she said.

Every time the choir assembled, Daddy would lobby Mother early and long, "Let's do my favorite song, 'When . . . '."

"Well, wait, Ab. You know we're going to get to it," Mother would appeal.

Daddy would eventually prevail, and we would all join him in his favorite—and our best: "When the Roll Is Called Up Yonder."

Daddy couldn't keep from exuberantly waving his arms and leading us in this one. He would always say as we finished, "I want that one done at my funeral." He said it so unvaryingly that we could lip-sync with him. And it was sung at his funeral.

Mother's Tabernacle Choir still assembles from time to time, without the original leaders, but with some promising apprentices. We still sing the oldies, mostly in the key of C. And we always do "When the Roll Is Called Up Yonder."

There is a strong hint of immortality present.♥

BURIED IN THE CORNFIELD

Sharon Lambert

It was a beautiful autumn morning; the leaves turning colors, the air crisp and cool. But inside our white two-story farm home the atmosphere was very different. I was getting dressed, ready to attend the one-room country school that my brothers and sisters had attended before me.

Mother was helping me put on the brace that I wore to correct the curvature in my spine. I was in a bad mood. Not only did I not want to wear the brace, I didn't like all the challenges this new school year was presenting.

That morning my vocabulary centered around two words: I can't. Finally, my mother had heard "I can't" one time too many. She looked at me and said, "I don't want to ever hear you say 'can't' again. 'I can't' died last night, and your dad and I buried him in the cornfield."

Years later, it was this same mother who kept saying "Yes, you can" when I thought getting a master's degree in teaching was just a dream. It was this mother who stood up and clapped for me as I walked across the stage on the day I got my graduate school diploma. Although the president of the college had said to wait until all names were called before applauding, it was this mother —who never breaks rules—who stood as my name was read and led my little group of five in standing beside her and clapping. When I asked her later why she had done it, she hugged me and said, "Because I knew you could do it. You're my daughter, and I love you."

It was these memories that filled my mind as I walked into my mother's hospital room on a cold, dark February afternoon. Mother had suffered a stroke two weeks earlier. She was paralyzed on the right side and was in much pain. She knew she was going to a nursing home. Tears fell from her eyes and ran down her cheeks.

I wiped her tears and held her hand. "Mother," I said, "we have to try to remember the happy times and think of the good times yet to come."

She squeezed my hand and cried softly, "I can't. I just can't."

Then, tenderly, I reminded her of the husband of 71 years who still loved her dearly, of the six children, the grandchildren, and the great-grandchildren who cherish her, and of the two great-grandchildren whose birth the family was still awaiting.

But most of all I reminded her of the time, years ago, when "I can't" died and was buried in the cornfield. ♥

SOME THINGS WE MUST ALWAYS BE UNABLE TO BEAR

Joe Kogel

I was watching television with my wife, Susan, and this story came on about a woman whose son was on Pan Am Flight 103, which blew up over Scotland killing all 259 aboard, most of them Americans. Many were students at Syracuse University returning from a semester abroad.

The mother who was profiled on the TV piece is creating a series of sculptures called Dark Eulogy. As part of her work she interviews the mothers of the students who died on that flight and takes each one back to the moment of finding out about the crash and that her child had been killed. Not one has ever forgotten exactly what she felt and what she did in that instant. Each has posed in the naked astonishment and unbearable grief of hearing the news.

One of the mothers who posed was the one

who appeared on film at the time of the crash, live, at the airline terminal gate. She had gone to wait for her child. When she heard about the crash she fell flat on her back, howling, "My baby, my baby!" As I watched her agonized writhing, I began to sob spontaneously. Later I connected my response to an awareness of how my own mother must have felt when she heard the diagnosis of my malignant melanoma.

At that moment I was aware of the profound vulnerability every parent must endure—the vulnerability each of us who contemplates parenthood must confront. I reached over to Susan. Touching her was a silent way of saying, *Are we ready for this? Knowing that such loss can occur, are we ready to love this way?*

When you conceive, intentionally or not, you don't imagine that your child will suddenly be snatched from you in 20 years by a terrorist bombing. But if you hold that possibility in your mind as you choose to make a new life and care for it, you become heroic by loving in the shadow of loss.

I know some people just want to forget. They turn the channel. They can't let it in. I do that, too. I listen to sports as a way to forget about the world for awhile. But tonight television is providing a rare glimpse of the self beneath the public self. These sculptures and screams, if they were the only pure thing ever aired, would be reason enough for TV to exist.

It is not for me to make sculptures of mothers. That is the homage of the woman who does. But I borrow the grief that fuels her work. I use it to drive a wedge into my careful forgetting, my imagined impenetrability. I wonder, what is my Pan Am 103? I wonder, is there an homage that I'm avoiding?

Using that question as a mantra moved me East, because my mother is mortal, my wife's parents and grandmother are mortal.

Cancer was a Pan Am 103 for me. I walked away from that crash, but the crash—the disease—will never leave me and, like a storm reaching into arthritic tissue, stories like the mothers of Pan Am 103 will always make me ache.

"Aren't you supposed to put your grief behind you—to get on with your life?" Charley Kuralt asked the sculptor/mother.

"We have gotten on with our lives," she said. "Dark Eulogy isn't the only thing I do. But my son's death will never stop being painful. Never."

She made no apologies. She didn't have to. She knows that Robert Frost was right when he said, "Some things we must always be unable to bear."♥

IV.
GRAND-
PARENTS

A MASTER TEACHER

Chick Moorman

Grandpa Brown never tried to influence my life. Perhaps that's why he was so effective at doing it. He didn't preach. He didn't scold. He drew no lines of right and wrong. He was content to live his life in ways that he determined best for him, and he let others do the same—me included.

Grandpa liked to bowl, and he enjoyed taking his grandchildren with him. Years before bowling became respectable, he'd surprise my brother and me with a Saturday trip to the bowling alley. It was in 1950, during one of these unexpected Saturday treats, that I was first exposed to an important notion that later became central to my way of living.

I remember being puzzled by my grandfather's reaction to splits. In bowling, a "split" is the event in which two or more pins remain standing on opposite sides of the lane, so picking up a spare becomes utterly impossible.

I hated splits and disowned responsibility for their occurrence. They were bad breaks, unlucky pin action, fate. No doing of mine. They brought my score down and were therefore undesirable. Grandpa Brown enjoyed splits. He smiled at every chance he got to roll at one. He actually looked forward to them! I noticed the discrepancy between our views on splits, and I asked him about it. His exact words are gone now, but I remember his attitude.

"How many times do you get a chance at a tough split?" he would ask.

"Too many," I would think.

His view was this: During every game he got plenty of chances to roll at all the pins, plus some shots at less challenging spares. The tough splits were the ones that didn't occur too often, so he didn't have many opportunities to test his skill against them. He appreciated their infrequency and anticipated their occurrence. He loved the challenge of the unusual and the flavor of the unexpected.

I would see a split and perceive it as potential, if not probable, harm to my score. I was tuned into the importance of the product—the end result. Grandpa saw splits as an opportunity to try something new, an opportunity to pit himself against unfamiliar circumstances. He was tuned into the importance of the process—the joy of participation. He liked to get high scores, too, but he placed greater value on the chance to participate and the adventure of the experience.

Grandpa Brown helped me experience the excitement of the process—of focusing on the notion that you don't have control over the splits that occur in your life, but you do have control over how you perceive them.

Above all else, my grandfather showed me the power of teaching by example. He modeled his messages. Because he didn't "teach," he taught.

Grandpa Brown never tried to influence my life. But he did.♥

GRANDMA'S LAW

Mike Buettell

When I was about five years old, my parents would take me to my grandmother's house in Pasadena, California. My grandmother was one of those wonderful women from a bygone era who would greet me at the door with a huge smile, throw her arms around me, and hug me so hard I thought my eyes would pop out of their sockets. I loved it. She would then lead me into the kitchen and, while telling me stories of times past, cook one of those magnificent "old time" dinners—you know, the cholesterol-nightmare type with lots of juicy red meat, gravy, mashed potatoes, gobs of real butter and cream and—of course—a wonderful, rich dessert.

Her meals were legendary. The smells alone were worth writing poetry about. Everything she cooked was superb—with one exception. Vegetables. She loved vegetables. I hated vegetables. And she cooked lots of them.

On one particular occasion, when it was time for dinner my father put three phone books on a dining room chair and invited me to join "the big folks" at the table. The meal was served, and it was extraordinary in every respect except one. There were vegetables on my plate. Not just any vegetables, mind you, but my three least favorite: brussels sprouts, cauliflower, and broccoli.

I quickly devoured the rest of my meal and sat quietly waiting for dessert to be served. My grandmother noticed that the vegetables sitting on my plate were untouched and asked me if I were going to eat them. Out of the corner of my eye I noticed an expression on my parents' faces which clearly said, *Mike, don't even think about making a scene here! Eat those vegetables, NOW!*

However, I was a stubborn child, and I politely told my grandmother, "I don't like brussels sprouts, cauliflower, and broccoli."

The air was as thick as country cream. My parents were mortified. I fully expected to be banished to the garage for the next 20 years. But my grandmother simply looked me straight in the eye and gave me one sentence of profound wisdom, a sentence that I've remembered for 40 years. She said, "If you eat your vegetables, you can have your dessert."

Well, I was outraged! I should get my dessert. I was special; I was her firstborn grandson. I wanted dessert and I wanted it now!

Calmly, my grandmother repeated what I've since come to refer to as "Grandma's Law": *If you eat your vegetables, you can have your dessert.*

I knew I was in trouble. This was a predicament unparalleled in my young life. I truly hated those vegetables, but I loved my grandmother's desserts. And my favorite—

homemade apple pie—was sitting on the counter less than two feet away. The smell alone was driving me crazy.

I looked at the vegetables. I looked at the dessert. And with sweat dripping off my brow, I slowly ate the now cold and rubbery brussels sprouts, cauliflower, and broccoli that remained on my plate. Chewing wasn't bad, but swallowing was a test of true willpower.

A lot of years have passed, but the simple lesson my grandmother taught me persists.

As a school counselor, I often encounter students who ask me how they can improve their grades. I reply, "If you eat your vegetables, you get your dessert." They look at me as if I'm crazy. So I translate and tell them that if they do their homework, study hard for tests, pay attention in class, and ask for help on things they don't understand, their grades will improve.

Sounds like "Grandma's Law" to me.♥

LETTING GO

Jessica Hill

Mourning doves have landed on the ledge outside my window. Already the sun is full. The air has a late-summer smell. I hear Mom in my grandfather's room, waking him. Then she comes in to me, saying it's time to be with Grandma.

One nurse says she doesn't know us. Another says she can hear us but might not understand. I open the curtains wide, letting in the morning light.

We take turns holding her hands. More children arrive. The hours pass. We watch her struggles lessen.

I think she senses us there, saying good-bye, and when the little room is filled up with all the love and hope it can handle, she knows it is okay to let go. Together we watch her chest quietly rise for the last time. We stare at the stillness until we understand that she has gone.

We cry because she has left us and because we know she had to go and because there are so many things that have been left unsaid. We cry for ourselves and for all those who never knew how her smile could light up a room.

We were the lucky ones. She gave us life, and the pain we feel now is worth the happiness we had then.♥

A DIFFERENT LIFE

Dexter Schraer

As youngsters on my grandfather's farm, about five miles south of Hermann, Missouri, my brother and I brushed our teeth with collapsible toothbrushes, baking soda, and well water—water as cold outside in summer as the bedsheets inside were in winter. We also walked along a foot-wide path to an outhouse which was humbling in daylight and terrifying enough for Stephen King, Clive Barnes, and Dean R. Koontz in moonlight.

For the last ten years of our grandmother's illness, we sweated each summer in the hayfields. Dirty, dusty, and disheveled, we learned to appreciate cleanliness and a cold bath or rinse after a day in the fields. Showers didn't exist on the farm.

We learned the pure and simple wonder of a cup of cold water. We learned the uses of red bandannas. We learned how to conserve energy while working hard. We learned the value of physical labor, sweat, and devotion from a man whose callused hands never knew gloves, no matter the time of year or the temperature.

Most of all, though, we learned to appreciate a man at peace with himself.

We never knew whether our grandfather was always as imperturbable as he was around us. To this day we wonder, especially in December, the month of his birth, how he responded almost 60 years ago to the telegram from a doctor in Columbia which read: "Upon examination of the dog's head, we find evidence of rabies. You should seek medical attention."

We wonder how he responded to our grandmother's illness, especially after he realized that his wife of more than 40 years would no longer walk or talk or travel to town or visit in church, but would linger, bedridden, on the edges of life for decades. His heart was so full of love that he cared for her, by himself, for almost 20 years.

We wonder how he responded to the sale of his farm—and to the nursing home.

We wonder, at times, about such matters. But we know this: Some men live young and die old. Some live old and die young. A few live fully until they die. Our grandfather chose the last of the three options.

I miss the well water—colder and sweeter than time itself. I miss the outhouse. I miss my grandfather who was, and is, still a part of my family, though he's been dead for years. And I sometimes long for the world in which he lived.♥

THE WINDOW OF MY ROOM

Kim Namenye
Age 11

The window of my room
is shining bright
because it lets in all the light

The window of my room
portrays a nice sound
when birds are singing all around

The window of my room
allows in a summer breeze
and blocks out a winter freeze

The window of my room
gives me all these wonderful gifts
and allows my thoughts to drift

The window of my room
has love and care
because my grandpa helped put it there♥

GRANDMOTHER'S CHRISTMAS
(Written Christmas Week, 1968)

Mildred H. Walton

Many definitions have been given of a grandmother, but the one I like best is: a grandmother is a woman who is either exhausted or lonesome. Right now I am exhausted, but soon I shall be lonesome.

My Christmas season started six weeks ago, when my son-in-law, Bob Ziegler, brought his little family to New Orleans to stay with us while he studied in Houston, Texas. I wondered if I would have the physical strength and the mental fortitude to cope with our daughter, Mildred, and her two and one-third babies. Sometimes a young mother wants and needs to be babied, and I am just the one to give her that extra love and attention. How wonderful to be needed!

In a few days all I shall have will be happy memories stored away in my heart of hearts. Our movies and slides will help a little, but they cannot take the place of a juicy kiss and two short arms around my neck. The other day Robert, who is four years old, was sitting on my lap counting my wrinkles when he gave up and said, "Grandmother, you have lots of wrinkles and you look like an old lady girl, but I love you just the same."

Grandchildren in the home make a few changes in your daily schedule. Privacy? Who expects privacy? A closed door means something interesting is going on behind that door. First comes a gentle rattle of the door knob, followed by quietness on both sides of the door. Then soft baby breathing, with another tug at the knob. "Grandmother? What are you doing?" I might as well open the door. The little one will not take the hint and go away. So into the bathroom he comes. Personally, I'm not interested in watching someone brush her teeth, but our little boys are fascinated by my bridgework and WaterPik.

In these troubled times, when some young people wonder who they are, where they are, and what they want to do with their lives, it is refreshing to have one as young as Robert know the answers to these questions. He knows he is Robert Henry Ziegler, Jr. He knows he lives in Pine Bluff, Arkansas, in a home in a neighborhood where people love him. He knows that when he grows up he wants to be a grandmother so he can take out some of his teeth.

I'm sure that whoever invented the word "babysitter" never sat with two such live wires as Robert and Aubrey. Their vitamins are more potent and effective than mine and their grandfather's.

During these last few weeks I have longed for an uninterrupted nap. In the quietness of the days to come, I wonder if I can possibly enjoy one. I think I shall miss Robert bumping against my night table—"accidentally" on purpose, of course —leaning on my bed, looking straight into my eyes, and asking if I am asleep. I am so glad I can look back and remember that not once was I cross with him for waking me from a nap of five minutes' duration.

When our dear ones crowd into their car, sitting on top of their gifts and goodies, I know I shall rush back to the family room and put my weary feet upon the ottoman to rest. My eyes will be moist only because I am tired, you understand.

I shall have to work hard and fast to put out of sight objects used by the children. Tears will come to my eyes as I notice the chairs in the dining room still draped with an old blanket. For a week or two it was a tent, but after one of the stories read from a library book, it became a covered wagon. Two little boys spent many happy hours in it driving two little stick horses across the wilderness. Who would have thought those old corrugated boxes from the grocery store would make such safe and sturdy boats? For weeks the children sailed across the family room floor without a single mishap.

God has been so good to me, giving me a wonderful husband, fine children, and precious grandchildren. Yesterday Robert said, "Grandmother, you look tired." Who wouldn't get tired carrying around so much happiness?

Going-home day has finally come. Our loved ones have left. As a rule the children are not allowed to lean out of the car, but this was a special occasion. I could not see for the tears, but I knew a little blond and a little brunette were waving little arms like windmills, throwing big kisses to us.

They have been gone 45 minutes. I suppose the children have opened one sack of toys. Although it is still early, I think Robert and Aubrey will be asking for the lunch I put up for them.

I am not very tired. Not nearly as exhausted as I thought I would be. But I am already lonesome.♥

HOW TO MAKE A GRANDMOTHER CRY

Sharon Lambert

The story begins in 1913—78 years before it ends—with the gift of a small ball to a little girl. Each day, as eight-year-old Mildred played with the new ball, she thought about how blessed she was. She and her brother, Jim, had a loving home with Uncle Joe and Aunt Emma, who had cared for them since their mother's death in 1907. And now she had this wonderful new ball. Red, yellow, and blue, it was, with pictures of playing children on both sides. Her joy was unbounded.

Uncle Joe and Aunt Emma were building an addition to their farm home at the time, and there was a crack, six or seven inches wide, between the old and new sections. One day when Mildred was playing with her new ball, it bounced and rolled into the crack and under the floor.

She cried, but she didn't ask for a new ball. Even at eight, she knew that money was tight, and playthings were scarce and hard to come by.

Mildred and Jim grew up and had families of their own. They often got together and talked about their childhood days and about the house where they had grown up and known such love. News of its razing, in 1991, prompted once again the sharing of memories, and Mildred told the story of the ball and its loss. She had never forgotten it.

Mildred's children got in touch with the old house's owner. Had they, by any chance, found a certain object beneath the floorboards while the house was being torn down? They had, indeed.

Sometimes it's very hard to keep a secret, but not that Christmas Eve. Over 60 family members gathered, cameras ready, to watch as Santa gave unsuspecting, 81-year-old Mildred a very special package. She opened it and, for a puzzled moment, just looked at the still vividly colored ball with the pictures of playing children on the sides. Then the memories came back and, with them, tears of joy and gratitude.

Seventy-eight years after it was lost, the ball was finally where it belonged, in the loving hands of its owner.♥

GRANDMOTHER'S JOURNAL

MaryAnn Faubion Kohl

A little lined, black-and-white composition book filled with my grandmother's thoughts was recently discovered in a box of old things. It has not been read by anyone except her since she wrote it 51 years ago.

I was not yet born when my independent-thinking, brave grandmother took her retreat to Orcas Island. Now, as I approach my 50th birthday, I find that my grandmother and I had much in common. Because she died when I was only ten, this personal diary of her thoughts and feelings is the first time I have been able to meet with her, adult to adult, peer to peer, and share in her thoughts. She titles her journal:

MY RETREAT, SEPT. 30, 1944

Mary Wilson
Winslow, Washington

*I've always found if I follow my first
hunch I'll be right. I've had this "hunch"
for several months, but keep fighting it off.
But now my plans for a retreat to Orcas
Island are unchangeable. Unchangeable,
yes, because I have the conviction that it is
the only way out of a time when I am
running on empty. It may look selfish to
others, but it is the most gracious and
unselfish thing I have ever done for my
family. When peace of mind is gone and
nerves on fire, no one, not even your most
loved ones, should have to suffer with you.*

*I love life and the living of it by finding
so much to do to keep another surprised
and happy. I have ceased to do that, making
my presence, even my tone of voice,
unbearable to myself. After many sleepless
nights and trying without success to get
myself back, I have decided to go away,
leave the home that is the loveliest spot
I've ever known. I've tried to find a way to
back out of my decision, but each time I get
the feel of a way out, mental anguish and
jerky nerves wash over me all over again,
reminding me of why I decided to leave in
the first place. This is a must for me and for
my family.*

*I had "something" at one time that
caused my family to love me, to kiss me,
and prepare little surprises for me. They
haven't found that "something" for these*

past four months, for they no longer do these little things. I call them little things— they were anything but that. The little things were the big things and they are gone. Respect is such an important factor for people living together—not just doing favors, especially, but more—respecting each other's thoughts, feelings, ideas, and wishes. I think I need to feel just a little spoiled too, "made over" a little, to give me that warm calm of self-confidence. I need to know there is Somebody who will always love me, understand me, listen to me.

So, a retreat, to a hideaway, to get back what I let go—a retreat where no one suspects how far off the right road I've traveled. No one to criticize while I make amends with my soul and mind, while I patch up the worn-out places in my heart.

As I leave, I have gone through my thoughts a million times. I've counted my blessings, but that is no new habit for me. I've always thought that love draws unto itself all that is its own. I've felt, if we love, we give without asking or without saying, "I did such-and-such." Love is free and natural like the air, the tides. It's warm and potent and silent in all it gives. I think of love most as I leave Bainbridge Island, filled with the fragrance of salt air, the little sparkly lights of Seattle, like a fairyland, in the distance.

All these thoughts I write because I have come away. (Not gone away.) A retreat for me—a time to think and be. I'm not running away from a problem or my responsibility, though it is unusual for a woman to travel alone for pleasure. But I must be alone. When a part in our car or boat becomes worn and gives bad service, we fix it. That's what I'm doing. This retreat is my repair shop and it's on Orcas Island where time will hold sway on the state of my heart, mind, and soul.

Several days later

This little cabin holds all I need except my piano and my old slacks. I would rather never go home again. I could easily give up all the antiques, my home, my garden, because none of these things is mine—they only came into my possession. But I could not give up my children or my husband; we are a part of each other. Yet, if I'd never known them, I could easily live without them. Still, I can't imagine them not existing.

Later

I walked to the post office, the store, the dock, several miles in soft breezes, and gathered wild flowers for my mantle. I have them in a rusty tin can and they are dainty in colors, fragile in texture, rich in perfume—like fluffy balls of pink cotton and yellow tousle-headed toddlers. As I walked up the road with my gladsome posies for my cabin, I passed a seasoned old farmer. He stared at my flowers. I thought I heard him thinking, "These crazy city folks don't know weeds when they see them." Then I remembered my own gorgeous flowers at home—azaleas, gladiolus, tuberous begonias, lilies, petunias, geraniums, zinnias—nearly every flower you care to find in the seed catalogues. But these flowers on my mantle have grown by nature's grace, from rain and sunshine alone. No man to hoe them, fertilize the soil, or turn on the hose. I love them; they are so free, so natural, so beautiful.

Later

Time to return home. I called home and it seems best I return tomorrow. I can't say "good-bye" to all this. I have to come back again, when I can. The rest I feel could be a new way of life.

Home again

I've been home from Orcas for one full week. I was watching the little fish in our pond, and thought: a pool cannot be kept clean and sweet and renewed unless there is an outlet as well as an inlet. It is our business to keep the outlet open, and God's business to keep the stream flowing in and through us.

I feel renewed even a week later. I feel I have found my own understanding heart to share with my loved ones. My soul is rested. Today is the 13th of October, and it seems like my luckiest day. All clues point to a great day. I must be thankful that I have been cared for to the ultimate good for all. Time to think and be. Perhaps I can find that here at home. My rusty tin can sits in my potting shed filled with weeds, the most beautiful flowers in my garden.♥

TOO SOON

Lisa Marzetta Albrecht
Age 17

Dear God, this is a letter just for you
To tell you that you took my grandpa too soon!
He means so much to me and I need him here.
He always made me happy. It's just not fair.

I love him so much and I need him today.
Am I being selfish for wanting him to stay?
I know he suffered and he gave a good fight,
But you took him anyway. I don't think that's
    right!
I know he is happy, don't get me wrong,
I just miss his warm hugs that he gave me so
    strong!

God, is my Grandpa still dancing like he always
    did?
He was the best, you know, that ever lived.
And God, did my Grandpa go to the Cubs opener
    like he wanted to?
I sure hope so. He was their best fan, you know!

And God, could you ask my Grandpa if he was
able to see me in the play?
No; I already know, and he was proud in every
way!
You know they say my singing voice came from
him;
I can still hear him singing to me and in the
church choir he was in.

Dear God, could you please tell him to keep up his
funny and joking style
So I can always remember his tender, loving
smile?
And God, please tell him to think of me now and
then,
And remember that I'll be loving him until we
meet again.
Dear God, please tell him that I love him so,
And I'll always care for him more than he'll ever
know!
And, Dear God, this is a message specifically for
you.
Please, take good care of my Grandpa since you
took him much too soon!♥

FOR ISADOR

Joe Kogel

My father's father committed suicide in 1934. My father was 15 years old when he found him asphyxiated in his car. My grandfather had been quite wealthy at the time of the stock market crash. He went bankrupt, and when he was unable to get back on his feet, he took his life. I wrote this poem as a way of making a connection with the grandfather I never met but whose life— and death—influenced me deeply.

Isador, father of my father
whose hands once cradled my father's infant
    body,
whose cobblestone voice filled the avenues of
    my father's ears,
to resonate there, forever.

Isador, before you take your life,
invite me into that garage,
and after you've closed the door,
but before you turn to the ignition, speak to
   me.
I won't budge.
My decade won't miss me, Izzy.
I've got nothing but time and two ears
in this front seat with you.

And yes, you're right.
I am trying to suspend time.
I'm waiting for the footsteps of Hank,
one score years before he would sire me,
Hank, fifteen; the middle of three.
Hank will come, but Izzy, he's going to find
   you breathing this time.
He's going to find you breathing.

Tomorrow will bring work—you'll see.
You'll see men walk on the moon.
You'll see grandchildren, Izzy,
and one of them will be a storyteller.
And something about him will seem so . . .
   familiar.♥

V.

LESSONS

FORTY-FOUR HOURS

Chick Moorman

Forty-four hours. Friday night from 6 p.m. until Sunday at 2 p.m. That's the amount of time we have as weekend parents to make a difference, leave an imprint, and hopefully bump our children's lives in a healthy, helpful direction. Not much time. But, sometimes, time enough.

"I'm not going. Can't afford it," I heard my daughter, Jenny, tell her best friend one Friday night, barely into my 44 hours.

"Too bad," said the friend. "Lots of us are going."

"Where is this?" I asked, butting into the conversation.

"Germany," Jenny responded. "Most of the swim team is going."

"And you're not?"

"No. I'd have to try out, plus it's a lot of money. It costs a *thousand* dollars, Dad!"

Jenny's emphasis on the word "thousand"

helped me realize just how big that amount appeared in her 16-year-old head. She could have easily substituted the word "million" for "thousand" and it wouldn't have affected the tone or intent of her comment.

The teens abruptly changed the subject, so I filed the Germany topic away under the category of "things to bring up later."

"Later" came Saturday, when I caught Jenny alone in the kitchen. "Tell me about this Germany, swim team situation," I said.

"It's with the YMCA," Jenny replied. "You have to try out. Most of the kids on my high school team are going to do it. If you make the Y-KATS, you get to go on the trip to Germany at the end of the summer. It's ten days. I'm a good enough swimmer to make the team, but I'm not going to do it."

"Tell me more," I prompted her, sensing it wasn't my turn yet and that she had more on her mind.

"What do you mean?"

"How did you arrive at your decision, and how are you feeling about it?"

"I decided not to go because it costs so much, and I'd never be able to get a thousand dollars in time. And I'm feeling left out because all my friends are going."

"So you're bummed because you'd like to be in on it and you don't see a way to pull it off?"

"Right. And I'll feel worse when they go," Jenny said.

"Do you want to go?" I asked.

"Yes!" Her answer was quick and decisive.

"Then why don't you?"

"Dad, I know you don't have the money. Neither does Mom. It's only four months away. I can't get a thousand dollars by then."

"You sure?"

"Dad, it's a *thousand* dollars. If I baby-sat every night from now until then I couldn't get a thousand dollars."

At this point, I realized that Jenny wasn't seeing herself the same way I was. My perception of her was of a persistent, determined, 16-year-old who knew what she wanted and could figure out ways to get it. While it didn't matter to me whether or not Jenny chose to pursue this particular opportunity, it did matter that she perceive it as possible and herself as capable. So I pushed it.

"Jenny, there's no doubt in my mind that you can get that money together in time if you really want to go," I told my daughter.

"What?" she said. "What do you mean?"

"I'm saying I know you can do it."

"Do you really think so?"

"I'm sure of it. I know you, and once you set a goal and go after it, there's no stopping you. You always find a way to get what you want."

That slowed her down. "Yeah. I am kinda like that, aren't I?"

I pressed the point home. "You sure are. So think about it some more, and we can talk later if you want."

"Okay," she said, and off she went to do the important things teenagers do on Saturdays. If it ends here, I'm satisfied, I thought. Jenny doesn't have to go to Germany if she doesn't want to. I'm comfortable with whatever decision she makes. If nothing else, I've at least let my daughter know in clear terms that I see her as a determined, able young woman. Just one good "I see you as capable" message sent during my 44 hours of influence helps me feel good about my parenting. Anything in addition to this is a bonus.

The bonus arrived on Sunday. Jenny informed me she wanted to talk.

"Do you really believe I can find a way to go?" she began.

"Of course," I said, without hesitation. I'd been thinking about the situation in the interim. I decided I would show Jenny my support not only with encouragement and ideas but with a financial contribution.

"I don't think I can get the money," Jenny responded.

"Jenny," I said, "I want to help you pay for this trip if you really want to go. Here's what I'm willing to do. I'll match every dollar you earn for this trip. If you get five dollars baby-sitting, I'll match it. If you get ten dollars mowing grass, I'll give you another ten. If you get money as a gift for your birthday or Christmas, I won't match that; I'll match only the dollars you earn and save. I'm also willing to help you explore other ideas if that would be helpful."

Jenny took me up on both offers. Before she went home on Sunday night, she had a long list of possible jobs as well as increased confidence and commitment to her goal of raising a thousand dollars. Her list included baby-sitting

lawn care

laundry

grocery shopping

housecleaning

tutoring

catering

car washing

gardening

reading aloud

begging relatives

By the following weekend, Jenny had created and distributed a flyer to friends, relatives, and neighbors. "NO JOB TOO BIG OR SMALL," it proclaimed, and went on to inform people of her commitment, enthusiasm, and strengths as an employee. She explained her goal of going to Germany with the Y-KATS and asked for help. That same week she wrote personal letters to all her relatives telling them about her goal and plans and asking that any birthday or Christmas gifts be cash this one time only as a special favor and way of supporting her in something she cared deeply about.

When the calls came, Jenny responded. She baby-sat. She did lawn work. She baked cookies. She washed and folded clothes. She picked up black walnuts until her clothes and hands were equally black.

By the time she was finished, her efforts had cost me $516. She made the Y-KAT team, went to Germany with money to spare, and had an unforgettable experience.

But the story doesn't end there. After her return, during another of my 44-hour weekend parenting experiences, Jenny showed me the photos she had taken on her trip, explaining every detail. When she closed the final page of the photo album, she turned to me.

"Dad," she said, "I want to thank you for making this trip possible. You're the only one who believed in me. Everybody else discouraged me. They said I could never do it. You helped me see it was possible, and I appreciate it."

Weekend parenting, full-time parenting, single parenting—it doesn't matter. None of us gets enough appreciation. So I sat there, soaking up my daughter's every word. This one incident could keep me going for at least six months.

But Jenny wasn't finished. "I had more fun than anyone," she continued. "I had the best time of all my friends, and you're responsible."

"How so?" I asked.

"Most of my friends got a free ride from their parents. They had the trip totally paid for, and they didn't appreciate it. Some just took it for granted, and they complained the whole time they were there. I had to work for my trip. I enjoyed every minute of it because I knew what it took to get there, and I did it myself. Thanks for setting it up that way, and thanks for believing in me."

Forty-four hours. That's all the time we get as weekend parents. Not a lot, but—sometimes—time enough.♥

MOTHER'S DAY

Fran O'Connell

We've stopped for breakfast after church: my husband, the two kids, and me. It's Mother's Day, but that's not really why we're here. We're here mostly because no one has done the grocery shopping. Cait orders pancakes; Brendon orders scrambled eggs. They fuss, play with the silverware, spill water. Don asks the same question he always asks when we eat out: "Why do we do this?"

Three other people come in—two women and a man. They sit at the table next to us. They all look old. I don't pay much attention.

Our breakfasts come, and I reach over and start to cut Cait's pancakes. I'm annoyed at having to cut the damn pancakes for her. My elbow gets in the syrup. The butter won't melt, and she wants ketchup for her sausages. The ketchup won't come out, and I have to pound on the bottle. I think about how glad I'll be when she can cut her own pancakes and pour her own ketchup.

We eat breakfast in "parents with young children" mode. That means Don and I stuff ourselves in order to be done when the kids announce after approximately eight bites: "I'm full." Between mouth stuffings we issue the usual directives: "Be careful." "Don't spill." "Eat your breakfast." "Turn around."

Somewhere in the process of stuffing and directing, I'm drawn to the people at the next table. A very elderly lady, probably close to 90, is having breakfast with her son and his wife, who look to be 65 or 70 themselves. Their food arrives and the man reaches over to his mother's plate. "I'll cut the french toast for you, Mom. It will make it easier to eat," he tells her.

For a moment my vision shifts and I feel the rhythm and the challenge of being part of a family. The joy of being loved. The awesome responsibility that love demands. And I'm a little ashamed that I'm sometimes resentful of the "constantness" demanded of me.

I hope that if Cait ever has to cut my pancakes, I'm aware enough to tell her I know how she must feel.♥

I SAID IT COULDN'T
BE DONE

Rosita Perez

"Come out, Mom! You have to see this!"

I hesitate. Nothing could be that important. Besides, I'm very busy. I'm frying potatoes.

But they insist, so I reluctantly go outside— and find stretched across the sky, reaching from one end of the city to the other, the most magnificent rainbow I have ever seen. We squeal and point and express our wonder. We run around the block calling other kids outside to see this outrageous display that Nature is offering.

The eldest goes to get her camera, and I warn her that it's much too expansive a scene to capture with an Instamatic.

She ignores me.

Years later, looking through an old photo album, I come across an incredible picture of a rainbow, and I remember that day.

She got the entire thing by shooting four pictures and combining them perfectly—but she never showed it to me. I said it couldn't be done.

It's so enriching to be proved wrong.♥

SWEEPING SAND

Robert Roden

When my five children were young, a sandbox was standard backyard equipment. The problem is that it was messy. I was willing to endure the mess in the yard and even the inconvenience of having to pick up various sandbox toys when I was cutting the grass.

What really frustrated me was the kids' insistence on carrying sand into the garage for various "projects." Week after week I'd sweep up the sand in the garage and return it to its proper container, becoming more and more upset. Although I told them repeatedly to keep the sand out of the garage, they continually "forgot," and I kept sweeping.

Each week my anger intensified until one day, sweeping furiously—and venting my frustrations to myself equally furiously—an internal voice interrupted. It said, simply: One day you'll wish you had sand to sweep out of the garage.♥

DIRTY WORDS

Ed Frierson

I attended a "scrub, sand, and paint" elementary school. If someone scribbled on a wall, it was quickly scrubbed off. If someone carved a message into the top of a desk, it was sanded away shortly thereafter. If someone drew pictures or scrawled dirty words on the walls of the bathroom stalls, they were hurriedly painted over.

The high school in the community I grew up in was also a "scrub, sand, and paint" institution. It was only when I used bathrooms in restaurants and other public places that I caught glimpses of the kinds of offending messages and "artwork" that were so quickly and carefully blotted from the walls and desks in the schools I attended.

On one occasion, as a member of the freshman basketball team, I had a new experience. Arriving at a rival school for a game, I was directed to the visitors' locker room to change into my uniform. Mounted along the length of one entire wall of the dressing room was a galvanized metal trough that looked a bit like the feeding trough I had seen on my cousin's farm.

As I used the group urinal—in itself a novelty—I couldn't help but notice that this was *not* a "scrub, sand, and paint" dressing room. There were drawings and phone numbers and dirty words covering every inch of the wall in front of me.

Right at eye level was a thick, black line which extended along the wall the entire length of the urinal. I could see words scrawled at the very end of the line, but they were too far away to read, so, when I'd finished my "business," I walked to the end of the line. The words read

IF YOU CAN ✳✳✳✳ ABOVE THIS LINE →→→→ →→→→→→→→JOIN THE FIRE DEPARTMENT!

When I got home from the game that evening, I said to my mother, "You wouldn't believe the stuff that was written on the walls in the school's dressing room." She asked what I'd seen.

Encouraged by her curiosity, I continued. "Well, there was this big, black line right in front of my eyes when I used the trough they had instead of a toilet. It stretched the entire length of the wall and, at the end, there were some words." I hesitated and squirmed. I'd never said a dirty word to my mother. My face felt hot, and I knew I was blushing.

"So, what were the words?" my mother asked. I could tell she really wanted to know.

I blurted out the sinful line, fully expecting to have my face smacked. But, instead, my mother burst out laughing. "Oh, that's a good one," she said. "I'll have to tell that to your grandfather. He'll love it." She paused, then added, "Of course, you know your father isn't interested in this sort of stuff."

Then came something even more unexpected. "By the way," my mother said, "I noticed you were uncomfortable saying one of the words that was written on the wall. I don't blame you. I'm uncomfortable with dirty words, too. So I use the word 'teakettle' in their place. I'm not interested in most of the dirty stuff people write on bathroom walls, but if you ever see another really funny one, tell me about it and use the word 'teakettle.' I'll understand, and I'll pass it along to Pop" (my grandfather).

From that point on, "teakettle" became one of the most useful words in my vocabulary—and, later, that of my children. Interestingly, the schools they attended for the first eight years were "scrub, sand, and paint" places where walls and desks were generally spotless.

All my children played on school teams. One year, during the first week of high school basketball season, my daughters played a practice game at a neighboring school. Riding home after the game, one of them made a comment which struck a familiar chord: "You wouldn't believe the stuff that was written on the walls in the locker room."

I had an immediate flashback. Brimming with the anticipation of passing along my mother's wisdom and prepared for some shocking stuff, I said, "Really? What?"

My daughter replied, "I can't tell you everything, but my favorite was: 'Be a regular guy . . . EAT PRUNES!'"

I laughed with her before I said, "The other stuff—the stuff you think you can't tell me—it's probably because of the dirty words, right?" She blushed and nodded. So I introduced her to the teakettle ploy.

My son found his own use for the word. He became a high school baseball coach in California. His teams won several league championships, and he was named the state's Coach of the Year. His players had both good and bad days, but "Coach Eddie" was always proud of them. One day he told me the following story:

"I was in the third base coach's box when one of my players tried to race from first to third on a bunt down the third base line. It's a risky play and one that, if unsuccessful, can be a rally-killer. As my cocky speedster neared the bag, he attempted to slide. His heel spike nicked the dirt, his ankle was twisted, and his leg skidded to a stop with his foot just inches short of the base. The mess-up enabled the third baseman to dive back onto his foot with the throw from the first baseman. The umpire, hovering over the bag, yelled, 'YOU'RE OUT!'

"Up leaped my kid on one leg with a grimace on his face and, with a howl that could be heard on the nearby tennis courts, he yelled 'Aaawwwhhh TEAKETTLE!?!!!' The umpire whirled around and asked, 'Whaddidee say?' I said, 'It's a long story. It's not about you. It's about my grandmother.'"

Eddie says that each year he tells his team how they can avoid being tossed (thrown out of a game) by eliminating any dirty words they might be tempted to use and saying "teakettle" instead. They smirk and act as though he's weird, but no one on the team gets tossed for using dirty words.

He asked me to tell his grandmother. He was sure she'd be proud of him.♥

THINGS THAT GO BUMP
IN THE NIGHT . . .

Jane Bluestein

We had our first thunderstorm of the season a few days ago. In the dark, in the middle of the night, I sat wrapped in a quilt, watching the flashes of light and waiting for the crash of thunder to follow. There was something warm and peaceful in the midst of such turbulent weather—perhaps affirmation of the arrival of spring, my favorite time of year.

I wondered how I had come to actually enjoy an experience that had once terrified me. Often while I was growing up I found myself engaged in "reality wars" with the grownups around me, experiencing one thing and being told that something entirely different was going on. But when it came to my thunderstorm traumas, someone got it right. I remember being comforted and reassured. Yes, thunder was loud and scary; lightning was sudden and invasive. But I was safe. It was okay.

Paradoxically, being allowed to be afraid—not having to stuff my feelings or pretend to be brave—made the experience ultimately a little less frightening. It even became associated, strangely, with a feeling of protectedness. Even now, when the bigger and more sudden "bangs" occur—and here in New Mexico they occur quite frequently—I may pull the covers over my head, but it's usually out of annoyance at being awakened. I may get startled, I may still put my hands over my ears once in awhile, but I can somehow find a place in the midst of the noise that feels somewhat safe.

Having worked with children and, more recently, with educators, counselors, and parents, I've come to appreciate not only the value but the absolute necessity of validating a child's reality, of taking children seriously and helping them feel safe.

Nighttime can be a scary time for children. (Even some adults find the dark unsettling!) The shapes lurking in corners and the shadows on the wall are very real to them. Yet the greatest commitment to respecting a child's feelings is likely to waver when you're awakened at two in the morning by an announcement that there's a monster in the closet. It's certainly tempting to mumble, "Don't be silly. There's no such thing as monsters. Go back to sleep." Your four-year-old isn't likely to thank you for clearing up his distorted reality and trot peacefully back to bed.

A number of parents have shared with me techniques they have used to give their children a greater sense of control over their environment —and their fears.

"What would make you feel safe?" some ask. Once they've exhausted the child's less workable suggestions (one kid said they should move), they can usually come up with some ritual or routine that everyone can live with.

One mother filled an old window cleaner bottle with water and replaced the label with a sticker that said "Monster Spray." "This will get rid of any monster in this house and send it back to its own mommy and daddy," she told her son.

Another reported that before her twins get into bed they get the broom and sweep all the monsters into the garage. Other strategies include leaving the lights on in the bedroom or the hall, letting the dog sleep in the child's room, putting away all the scary clothes draped over the dresser, or putting a chair in front of the closet door. So long as the solution did not present problems for anyone else or keep others awake, most parents were open to just about anything.

The best solutions I've heard for dealing with a child's fears—or any feelings—included the parent's willingness to listen without judging or reacting in any negative way (with impatience or annoyance, for example) and to give the child the space and permission to simply have those feelings.

If we do our job well, one day our children may come to know that of all the gifts they have been given, the gift of trusting their own reality is the most precious of all.♥

DRESSED FOR SUCCESS

Mitch Anthony

I had just finished speaking to parents in a rural Minnesota town when I was approached by a man who obviously had something to say.

"Well, you sure made more sense than the last fella I heard speak!" he began.

"Why's that?" I asked.

"Like you, he was talking about children's self-esteem, but I'd like to know which college gave him that Ph.D. he's got. He told us that if a kid wants designer clothes a good parent should get them because the kid's self-esteem depends on it."

"Really?" I was surprised.

"Yep," he said. "I want you to know, I can't afford designer pants and shoes for my kids. But that don't mean they can't be proud of who they are. See, I'm a pig farmer, and I happen to know that pig crap looks the same on Kmart jeans as it does on Calvin Kleins. I'm not fooled one bit. I know it's not what I put on the outside of my kids that makes 'em feel good about who they are. It's what I put on the inside every single day."

In spite of his children's lack of designer clothing, they were, indeed, "dressed for success."♥

WE NEVER TOLD HIM HE COULDN'T DO IT

Kathy Lamancusa

When my son, Joey, was born, his feet were twisted upward, with the bottoms resting on his little tummy. Although this looked funny, as a first-time mother, I didn't know what it really meant.

What it meant is that Joey had been born with club feet. The doctors assured us that with treatment he would be able to walk normally. But they also told us he would probably never run very well.

The first three years of his life Joey spent in surgery, casts, and braces. His legs were massaged, worked, and exercised, and by the time he was seven or eight, if you watched him walk, you wouldn't even know he'd had a problem.

If he walked great distances, like at amusement parks or on a visit to the zoo, he'd complain that his legs were tired and that they hurt. We'd stop walking, take a break for a soda or ice cream cone, and talk about what we had seen and what we had yet to see. We didn't tell him why his legs hurt and why they were weak. We didn't tell him this was expected, due to his deformity at birth. We didn't tell him, so he didn't know.

The children in our neighborhood ran around a lot, as most children at play do. Joey would watch them and, of course, would jump right in and play, too. We never told him that he probably wouldn't be able to run as well as the other children. We didn't tell him he was different. We didn't tell him, so he didn't know.

In seventh grade he decided to go out for the cross-country team. Every day he trained with the team. He seemed to work harder and run more than any of the others. Perhaps he sensed that the abilities which seemed to come naturally to so many of them did not come naturally to him. We didn't tell him that although he could run with the team, he probably would always remain in the back of the pack. We didn't tell him that he shouldn't expect to be a team runner. The team runners are the top seven runners of the school. Although the entire team runs, it's only these seven who have the potential to score points for the school. We didn't tell him, so he didn't know.

Joey continued to run four or five miles a day, every day. One day he had a 102-degree fever. He couldn't stay home; he had to go to school for tests, he said. And then he had cross-country practice. I worried about him all day. I expected to get a call from the school asking me to come and bring him home. No one called.

After school, I went out to the cross-country training area, thinking that if I were there he might decide to skip practice. When I got to the school, he had already taken off on his route. I started to drive the route and found him running along a tree-lined street—all alone. I pulled up beside him and drove slowly to keep pace with him as he ran. I asked how he felt. "Okay," he said.

He had only two more miles to go. As sweat rolled down a face with eyes glassy from fever, he looked straight ahead and kept running. We never told him he couldn't run four miles with a 102-degree fever. We didn't tell him, so he didn't know.

Two weeks later, the day before the second-to-last race of the season, the names of the team runners were called. Joey was number six on the list. He had made the team. He was in seventh grade. The other six team members were all eighth graders.

We never told him he probably shouldn't expect to make the team. We never told him he couldn't do it, so he didn't know. He just did it.♥

31 FLAVORS

Jenny Moorman

I remember the day clearly. I had been working at Baskin Robbins. It was my first job, and I was required to wear a smock made hideous by its color. I wondered who could possibly be so color-blind as to choose brown, orange, and white stripes. As if that weren't bad enough, the smock was cut to show exactly what each adolescent ice cream scooper "had" or hadn't. I had, and, at 16, every time I put on that brown, orange, and white-striped smock, I became painfully aware of just how much.

That particular day I came home from work with my hated smock covered in ice cream. Mom thought it was a hoot and tactlessly pointed out how the chocolate, strawberry, and rocky road always seemed to find its way to my chest. I looked at her, with her slimmer, size B cup, and groaned. How could she possibly understand what a huge embarrassment this was?

I scrunched up my face, ready to protest. Then I changed my mind—and my battle plan. I became a clown. I began to describe how someone my height had to bend and stretch to scoop ice cream. I told how sometimes the place got so hot, everything melted. Was it my fault my body acted like some strange ice cream magnet? I groaned. I moaned. I animated the story as best I could. I wasn't going to let this get me down.

Mom smiled. Not a broad grin or a laugh. Just a simple smile. Her eyes reflected the smile, and she said, "You look like your father. You look just like your father did when I fell in love with him."

That was the moment I first knew that I was a child born of love—that I had character and charm. I knew I had inherited my father's expressions and wacky sense of humor, and I knew that I would outgrow this awkward, insecure stage. In fact, at that moment, I did.♥

THE EASY WAY OUT

Young Jay Mulkey

During my tenth summer I spent two weeks with my father and my uncle driving through Colorado, New Mexico, and Texas. We stopped mid-morning to fish in a clear mountain stream, stayed a couple of days in a cabin where we needed several blankets to keep us warm at night, and, in a very small town, took turns setting pins by hand so we could bowl. It was a time of high spirits and camaraderie but, in the end, painful consequences.

One morning toward the end of the second week, my father announced that if we started early and drove without stopping, we would be home that night. That meant we would have to endure the increasingly hot August weather only one day instead of two. (This was before cars were equipped with air-conditioning.) I quickly agreed because even the wind coming in the car windows was hot. We checked out of the motel and started for home.

About an hour later, I reached into the paper sack where I kept chewing gum, hard candies, and some souvenirs from the places we had visited. I took out an ash tray. Holding it at eye level, I inspected the name of the last motel we had stayed at. It was written in green letters across the inside of the ash tray.

"What's that you have there?" my father asked from the front seat.

"An ash tray," I replied.

"Where did you get it?"

My answer was glib. "From the motel."

"The motel manager give it to you?"

"Not exactly," I said.

Whenever we talked to each other on the trip, my father would look into the rearview mirror so he could see me. I could tell by his eyes that he was waiting for more of an explanation.

"Well, it was in our room."

"You didn't ask the manager for it, then?"

"He expects people to take ash trays. That's why it has the name of the motel on it. It's a way to advertise."

My father pulled to the side of the road, stopped the car, and turned around in his seat. "You took the ash tray *without* asking for it," he said. "We're going back to the motel, and you're going to return it to the manager."

I couldn't believe it! Surely he wouldn't drive all the way back just to make me return a cheap ash tray. That would add *two hours* to our driving! Suddenly, I had an idea. There was a way to get out of this.

"I'll mail it back," I said. "And I'll write a letter, too. Then we won't have to spend all that time driving back. You wanted to drive straight home. You can still do it."

"No." He started to turn the car around.

Desperate, I protested, "It's just a cheap ash tray. He probably has hundreds more. He doesn't need this one. That's a lot of trouble just to return a stupid ash tray."

"It's not the value of the ash tray, and it doesn't matter if he has hundreds," my father said. "And, yes, you *could* mail it back. But that would be the easy way. If you take the easy way out of returning, as you say, a 'cheap ash tray,' then you may want to take the easy way out again when you have to admit you did something wrong. Remember, cowards take the easy way out."

We went back.

Twenty-five years later my father's words came back. A good friend of mine and my wife was a hypochondriac. At least ten minutes of every visit we spent listening to a description of her latest ailment. After one visit I said to my wife, in front of my five-year-old son, "There's *nothing* wrong with her. She's as healthy as a horse!"

On our friend's next visit, after she had described her new ailment, my son said to her, "My father says there's *nothing* wrong with you, that you're as healthy as a horse!"

If there had been a hole in the floor, I would have gone through it—gladly. The only way I could think of to cover my embarrassment was to say, "He misunderstood what I said." But before I could say it, my father's words came back: *Cowards take the easy way out.*

Summoning my courage, I said instead, "He's right. That's what I said."

It is now many years later. Our friend is still a hypochondriac, but she is also still our friend. And I passed my father's legacy on to my son.

Cowards take the easy way out.♥

THE SIGNAL

Stan Dale

In my younger life, I was the kind of parent that I now decry, an authoritarian bully. I was narrow-minded and violent. I grew up in the ghettos of New York and fought to survive a street gang. I was trained to kill in Korea. I believed that my wife and children belonged to me. My attitude toward others was, *Don't you dare interfere if you value your body.* I didn't know better. I thought that was the way a father was supposed to be.

Then I began to study transactional analysis, and I learned there was a better way, a whole new world. I got valuable input from hundreds of thousands of people on my radio talk shows and in lectures and classes. A brand new world opened up for me.

I began to dread the role of authoritarian father. I couldn't stand the terror and pain in my children's eyes as they waited for the judge, jury, and executioner (me) to come home and address their wrongs. Slowly I began to change my parenting style, using my new transactional analysis tools.

I asked my family for assistance. I told them I simply wanted to love and enjoy them. I asked them to resist any harsh or unfair treatment. If they caught me acting like a bully or a dictator, they were to call me on it immediately.

Because my emotions often ran unchecked when discipline was called for, and because I was bigger, louder, and stronger than they, we devised a hand signal to act as a traffic cop for my runaway mouth. The signal, agreed upon for many reasons, was the peace sign.

Even though, as "Big Daddy," I had given them permission to "flip me off," they were still suspicious. They were not sure it would work. One day I was in the middle of giving Scott, who was about five or six at the time, a royal bawling out. Suddenly he ducked his head under his outstretched arm and gave me the signal. It stopped me like I had been struck by a bolt of lightning. In mid-sentence I started grinning, then broke into laughter. I grabbed Scott in my arms and hugged and kissed his frightened face until we were both laughing and crying. I held him for a long time and thanked him repeatedly. I told him how much I loved him and appreciated what he had done.

To this day I can't remember why I was so angry. It no longer matters. This was about the last time I used physical or emotional violence against my children or anyone else.

What I did wasn't magic, and it didn't work immediately. It didn't completely stop me from losing my temper, but it was a start. Like an alcoholic, I had to make an all-out commitment to my philosophy and follow through. It was a step-by-step, day-by-day process. My despised, toxic behavior changed over time, like any habit which is replaced with new behavior. Now I can honestly state that the habit is totally gone. I've been "clean" for over ten years.

Thank you, Scott, for helping lead the way. Peace!♥

MY OWN RAINBOW

Randi Curtiss
Age 14

Thanks to my family, I've learned that money isn't necessary for true happiness.

My father is self-employed, and looking back I can see how much I didn't have. But the thought never even occurred to me at the time. I always thought of myself as the luckiest kid alive. I had a windmill not ten feet outside my front door, even though the well was dry and it creaked noisily whenever the wind blew. I had a back porch, even though it was only the size of a picnic table and covered with green, fake grass. I had the large herd of ducks and geese that Mom kept in a pen behind the trailer. We used to let them out, then stand on the back porch and toss bread. They'd race all over, stealing bits off each other's pieces.

And I had my rainbow. In the small bedroom where the three of us kids were crammed together, there was a small window with a clear rainbow sticker on it. I used to sit for hours, staring at the wind-tossed prairie grass through the red, orange, and yellow, and watching the clouds turn colors as they passed through the curved bands of color.

We eventually moved into a house not 300 feet from where the trailer once stood, and I've never seen my rainbow since. Mom still has her poultry, but we took the windmill out because it was becoming dangerous to have around. I don't know what happened to the back porch.

We loaded the trailer onto a semi truckbed one day, and I waved good-bye to my home of five years. Now all that's left of the trailer is the perimeter of blue irises that grew around it. But I'll never forget what I learned about happiness living there.♥

THE TREE HOUSE

Leslie Stambaugh

When my daughter, Erika, was about seven, she came to me one day and started talking about a tree house and how much she'd like to have one. "You could go there when you wanted to be alone, you could use it as a clubhouse, you could have your friends there, you could . . . ," she went on excitedly.

I remembered how much I had wanted a tree house when I was a kid. And I really wanted to be able to give her one. And I knew I couldn't.

"Erika," I broke in. "I'm sorry, hon, but you can't have a tree house here. You know we don't even have a tree big enough to hold one!" I guiltily started to list all the reasons she couldn't possibly have a tree house when my daughter stopped me.

"I know all that," she said. "But I was just thinking about it and wanted to talk to you about how neat it would be!"

Sometimes our own defensiveness gets in the way of our listening to what is most important for others to share with us.♥

SELF-CARE FOR MAMAS

Marianne Preger-Simon

"Emily, would you please take your dolls out of the living room and bring them to your bedroom?"

Ten minutes later. "Emily, dear, how about taking your dolls out of the living room and into your bedroom?"

Another ten minutes. "Honey, I have an idea. I think you should take your dolls out of the living room and bring them to your bedroom."

Eventually. "Thanks, Emmy."

When I was a young mother, I had a fierce dread of being a nag. I didn't like the sound of nagging, I knew it wouldn't feel good to me, and I imagined it wouldn't be very pleasant for anyone else, either. I also had a sure sense that it was a very ineffective way of communicating. So I pondered the issue, determined to find a process that would be nurturing for me and leave the least amount of emotional garbage in my environment.

What I finally came up with was the concept of always asking my children to do something as if I had never asked before. Even if it were the tenth time I was making the request, I would say it as if it were the first. And I would engage the attention of my children with my own full attention before speaking to them.

What I remember most about this process was that it allowed me to feel good in my interactions with my children. I have no way of knowing whether it produced faster or better results than nagging would have, but I do know it was a wonderful way of creating the household atmosphere that I wanted—of taking care of myself while simultaneously making life more relaxed and pleasant for those around me. And that's the best kind of self-care of all.♥

ACCUMULATED DIVIDENDS

Rosita Perez

The kids grow up. We know we did our best. I don't know about you, but at no time did I ever wake up and think: What can I do to make their day miserable?

Yet, as I look back, I know I did. A certain look. A derisive comment. An impatient order. An angry scowl. An unfair decision. A time when what was needed was for me to listen, and instead I gave opinions. Often wrong.

One day, reminiscing around the kitchen table, I tell my daughters—three beautiful women now in their thirties—that I regret having been so rigid. That today I can live with a cluttered room. And an overflowing laundry basket. And unironed clothes waiting for the mood to strike me. It seldom does anymore.

She looks at me with enormous brown eyes. The one I most often showed my exasperation to when I found her doing things like looking for her shoes under the bed as the school bus approached—or building a fort out of an old bedspread so she could read by flashlight to our dog. She looks at me and says, with great tenderness: "Mom, you may not always have said or done the right thing, but it was okay because we knew you loved us. You always loved us. So the rest didn't matter."

Where did she learn such empathy? This was the kid who said to me, when I was in *my* thirties, "Remember how kooky you are, Mom. That way, when you're in your seventies you won't blame it on old age."

Express your misgivings and regrets to someone you love. Their compassion may surprise you.♥

A LITTLE BIT SMARTER

Andrew Proffitt
Age 14

Some people say that if you read to your kids when they're real young that they will become smart and successful when they get older. My parents must have heard that somewhere before they had me and my sister.

I remember my parents reading to me a lot when I was a young kid. I'd have to get a drink of water and then they would take me into my room and read to me. I remember Dr. Seuss and the Golden Books being read to me a lot. I never ran out of books for my parents to read to me because I had a whole library of them.

I truly believe that is what helped me to become a little bit smarter today. I know I didn't get my smartness from inheritance because, from what my parents told me, they got all Cs and Ds in school. So the only reason I can think of that I'm smarter is that my parents took the time to read to me when I was a kid.♥

"UNFORTUNATELY, WE'LL ONLY BE GONE FOR FOUR HOURS."

CAR TALK

Jane Stroschin

"Get in the car," I said, flashing a smile at my preteen son. "I have a surprise for you."

"What?" he asked.

"If I tell you, it's not a surprise."

We got in the car and drove off to the country. Why the country? No particular reason. The first time I offered him a "surprise" we drove to the new fast food place, for curly fries. The second trip was to a scenic lookout point to see the autumn colors at sunset.

Where we drive to isn't the important part of the story. Why we get in the car and drive anywhere is.

What I've discovered is that if I take turns inviting each of my children (one at a time) on a "surprise" trip periodically, *we talk*. Really talk. About everything: school, friends, religion, jobs, sex, politics. Actually, my kids talk. I ask questions and listen, occasionally interjecting a positive comment like, "I'm proud of you," or "I'm glad you're my son."

Maybe talking in the car is easier because you don't look at each other. Maybe it's because there is nothing else to do for the stretch of driving time there (wherever "there" is) and back. Whatever the reason, it happens.

And I discovered my kids enjoy it at least as much as I do. After my first few "surprises," they began coming to me, asking, "You wanna go for a ride?"

I drop whatever I'm doing, grab my car keys, and we're off.♥

WISHBONE

Kenneth R. Freeston

Deep beneath the skin of every roasted chicken is the one thing a child seeks. It holds the promise of a future filled with hope. It's the wishbone.

After how many childhood meals did my mother put the y-shaped, skinny, greasy bone on the windowsill by the kitchen sink, set there to dry overnight? The next morning she and I would each grab a side of the frail bone and pull. That was before I was old enough to know that by putting your thumb in the right place you could almost guarantee a win. Most times my mother let me win, although I didn't know that until years later.

David, my son, made his first significant wish last week. Chickens have been sacrificed in our house to buy hopes of better toys for some time now, but this wish was different. After breakfast, when the bone from the previous evening's dinner had dried, he snapped it and smiled at the long piece in his five-year-old hand.

"I wished I'd never be angry again, Mom," he announced.

David's own anger at wants unmet is more of a concern to him than we had realized, and we were more than a little relieved to see that he wanted no more of that stuff. It lasted less than an hour, this anger-free state, when a friend stopped by before school and the two of them fought over how the drums were to be played.

Later, at bedtime, his mom asked David if he remembered his wish from the morning. "Yes, Mom," he replied. "And sometimes it takes a long time for a wish to come true, doesn't it?"♥

ENCOURAGEMENT 101: NURTURING CONFIDENCE

Jane Bluestein

On the bulletin board in my office hangs a two-inch round button with an illustration of a train engine encircled by the words, "I think I can. I think I can." Of all the stories that were read to me when I was very young, I think my all-time favorite was—and still is—*The Little Engine That Could*. I owe a great deal of my adult success to the message I got from this book and from my family, the members of whom all seemed to have the idea that I was capable of doing or learning just about anything.

Maybe it was because I was the first child and the first grandchild on one side of the family. I don't know. But my earliest memories are of an attitude that reflected back to me a sense of my own competence, an appreciation for my curiosity, and a great deal of support in exploring a variety of interests, particularly in the areas of art, music, cooking, and crafts.

My parents were encouraging almost to the point of indulgence. Whenever I expressed an interest in something, the necessary supplies, materials, equipment, or instruments would almost magically appear. They would either demonstrate how to do things or provide me with the necessary classes or instruction. They never questioned my ability to excel at any of the numerous ventures I wanted to explore. As a result, I have a great deal of confidence in just about any endeavor I'm tempted to undertake and believe that, with very few exceptions, I am capable of learning and achieving just about anything.

Nonetheless, I've certainly had experiences that attempted to unravel this confidence, and I've run into my share of people who relished exploiting my vulnerability when I wasn't particularly good at something. (A couple of gym teachers come to mind.)

So, in addition to a belief that *I can*, there are also these *you can't* voices that pop up on occasion to accuse me of everything from having too much chutzpah to being a complete fraud. Despite feeling thoroughly grounded in a belief in the work I'm doing, I sometimes encounter a "committee" in the back of my consciousness, asking "Just who do you think you are?" especially when I sit down to write or stand up to speak to an audience. And any time I go to my health club to work out I have to do business with my eleventh-grade P.E. teacher, whom I can't seem to get out of my head.

But I go nonetheless. And I keep writing and speaking. I'm willing to "show up." In spite of all the "committee" chatter that sometimes clouds my head, those earlier *I can* voices still ring louder, clearer, and more true than any of the voices of doubt.

I believe in the power of those early, positive messages—the ones that have always been there saying, "I believe in you"—reflecting back to me a picture of myself that was bigger and brighter than anything I could have imagined. This is the information that empowers me to turn down the volume on the "committee's" all-static channel and counter with confidence: I knew I could! I knew I could!♥

A MEMORABLE DAY

Karyn Buxman

"I can't do that." "I'm not smart enough." "I'm too slow." "My hair is ugly." "Jacob says I could eat an apple through a picket fence." "I hate my freckles."

I was alarmed at the amount of negative self-talk coming from my own two kids. Where in the world were they getting those kinds of messages —and what could I do to turn them around?

I didn't want my sons growing up ingrained with such destructive messages, so I devised a plan. Whenever I heard them use a self-judging negative phrase, I would flash them a hand signal. They would have to stop mid-sentence and repeat the following aloud: "I'm very smart, I'm very talented, I can do anything I put my mind to, and I love myself."

The response was usually predictable. They would roll their eyes, let out a sigh, and recite as instructed, typically lacking any enthusiasm. But it usually derailed their pessimistic thoughts and they would move on to something else, sometimes even with a hint of a smile.

A year passed, and the need for the exercise seemed to diminish, but I wondered sometimes if it had really helped or if my sons were merely keeping negative comments to themselves. One hot and hectic summer morning I got my answer.

It was day three of a week-long national conference that I co-chaired in my own hometown. The kids sat in front of the TV, engrossed in cartoons while I showered and mentally reviewed the day. *The first speaker begins at 9:00 so I'll get there by 8:30, make announcements at 8:45, then introductions . . . but what if the conference starts earlier today?*

I shook the thought from my head. Of course, it doesn't start earlier today. I would have remembered something that important. I began the review again. *The first speaker begins at 9:00 so I'll get there by 8:30, make announcements at 8:45, then . . . but what if it did start early today?* Surely, I wouldn't forget something so important. Or would I?

I wrapped a towel around me and dripped all the way to the phone. I'll call Cyndi (the other co-chair) and straighten this out, I thought. Cyndi's husband answered the phone.

"Hello, Andy," I said. "Let me speak to Cyndi."

"She left about 30 minutes ago," Andy replied. "You know the schedule starts an hour earlier today."

I dropped the phone. "Boys!" I yelled, frantically. "Get your clothes on and grab some breakfast!"

"There's nothing to eat," the nine-year-old hollered back.

"Ding Dongs and Twinkies in the bottom cabinet! Move it!" This didn't seem to be the time for a lecture on proper nutritional choices.

I raced back to the bathroom, threw my clothes on, pulled my hair back, and slapped makeup on my face. I was shocked. "How could I have done something like this?" I muttered to myself. "How could I be such an idiot? I'm in charge. What kind of leader am I? Who in the world thought I could do this? I'm too stupid to be in charge. Only an idiot would screw up like this . . . "

Totally caught up in belittling myself, I was oblivious to the fact that my two sons were observing me from the bathroom door. "Stop," the six-year-old said as he placed his hands around my face, turning it toward his own. "You're very smart, you're very talented, you can do anything you put your mind to, and we love you!"

Shaken back to reality, I began to laugh. I hadn't even been aware of my own destructive conversation with myself. And then I hugged them back in delight. They got it! They understood my lesson well enough to teach it back to me.

I didn't get to the conference in time to make the announcements or even to introduce the morning speaker. It didn't change the earth's rotation. But it turned out to be a most memorable day—thanks to my sons.♥

TADPOLES, TRANSFORMATION, AND LETTING GO

Cecelia J. Soares

It was about the size of a quarter and it was quite green and it taught me one of my most important lessons about life and parenthood when I was only three years old.

We found it on a bright April Sunday. My mother and father and I had gone on a picnic, and my dad took me to a small, languid stream where we discovered a lively group of tadpoles, flickering and flashing in the water. I was so excited! Dad hurried back to the picnic site to find a container, and together we captured one of the little creatures. He let me think I had done it myself, and I brought the jar back to my mother with great pride. Knowing now how she feels about worms, bugs, and reptiles, I'm touched and impressed by how convincingly she shared my excitement and praised "my" accomplishment.

When we got home, my mother put the tadpole in a fishbowl and my parents told me that something wondrous and amazing would happen to him. I didn't really understand what they were talking about—I suppose I thought he was some sort of fish—but in a few days the tadpole began to develop little legs and then, a few days later, little arms. Then its tail began to disappear and its eyes began to bug out and it turned green.

One memorable morning, as I climbed up on the kitchen counter to see him, finally a frog, he leapt out of the bowl, through the unscreened window, and vanished into the green grass outside.

I was devastated. I sobbed uncontrollably. My frog was gone.

My mother took me outside and we searched in vain for the frog. He was small and green, and the grass was green. It was hopeless. I sank disconsolately into the grass, bereaved and worried about my wondrous little friend.

I remember my mother taking me in her arms to comfort me. She assured me that the frog would survive—that, in fact, he probably would have died if we had kept him confined. She talked in language I could understand about how he needed to be free—how it was his nature and his destiny and how, if we lock things up, even out of kindness, past their need for our care, they wither and die, killed by our misguided love.

The next day we went to the pet store and I picked out a goldfish.

As I grew older, I had a number of pets, majored in zoology at the university, and went on to become a veterinarian. I'm not sure how much of a role the little frog played in those choices, but

I do know how profoundly I learned that early lesson about letting go—about how we can actually harm something we love by hanging onto it.

As my own children came along and grew up, I revisited that powerful childhood incident often. My children are now 18 and 23. They don't know it, but as they passed through their various stages of growth, development, and transformation, I was a little more able to let them go because of a small green frog.♥

THE ALL-LEATHER, NFL REGULATION, *1963 CHICAGO BEARS*-INSCRIBED FOOTBALL

Tom Payne

The year was 1964. The place was Chicago. A man I worked with had acquired a couple of all-leather, NFL regulation, *1963 Chicago Bears*-inscribed footballs and was selling them at a real good price. My first son was on the way. (This was in pre-ultrasound days, but I figured we had a 50/50 chance it would be a son. It was a chance I was willing to take.) I bought the football. I had my son's "coming home from the hospital" gift, and it was something truly special.

Several years later, young Tom was rummaging around in the garage as only a five- or six-year-old can rummage when he came across the all-leather NFL regulation, *1963 Chicago Bears*-inscribed football. He asked if he could play with it. With as much logic as I felt he could understand, I explained to him that he was still a bit too young to play carefully with such a special ball. We had the same conversation several more times in the next few months, and soon the requests faded away.

The next fall, after watching a football game on television, Tom asked, "Dad, remember that football you have in the garage? Can I use it to play with the guys now?"

Eyes rolling up in my head, I replied, "Tom, you don't understand. You don't just go out and casually throw around an all-leather, NFL regulation, *1963 Chicago Bears*-inscribed football. I told you before; it's special."

Eventually Tom stopped asking altogether. But he did remember, and a few years later he told his younger brother, Dave, about the all-leather, NFL regulation, *1963 Chicago Bears*-inscribed football that was special and kept somewhere in the garage. Dave came to me one day and asked if he couldn't take that special football and throw it around for awhile. It seemed like I'd been through this before, but I patiently explained, once again, that you don't just go out for no reason and throw around an all-leather, NFL regulation, *1963 Chicago Bears*-inscribed football.

Soon Dave, too, stopped asking.

A couple of months ago I was in the garage looking for some WD40 (which, with the aid of a rubber hammer, I use to fix everything I choose to fix), when I noticed a large box that had "coveralls" written across it. I couldn't remember bringing along any coveralls when we moved from Chicago to Albuquerque, so I opened the box. And there, long forgotten, was the all-leather NFL regulation, *1963 Chicago Bears*-inscribed football.

But it wasn't special anymore.

I stood alone in the garage. The boys had long since moved away from home, and suddenly I realized that the football had never been so special at all. Children playing with it when it was their time to play is what would have made it special. I had blown those precious, present moments that can never be reclaimed, and I had saved a football. For what?

I took the football across the street and gave it to a family with young kids. A couple of hours later I looked out the window. They were throwing, catching, kicking, and letting skid across the cement my all-leather, NFL regulation, *1963 Chicago Bears*-inscribed football.

Now it was special!♥

VI.
HEROES

A BIG OLD GRIN

Ann Tait
Age 14

Sometimes the lessons that you learn in life come from the people you least expect it from. My little brother, Jimmy, is 12 years old. He's also mentally and physically handicapped. He had a stroke before he was born, and parts of his body (his toes and his brain) didn't completely form.

But even though those things aren't completely what they should be, I think Jimmy made up for it in the area of his heart. When we go out in public, there are people who stare at us, who won't even come near us, because they're afraid—afraid of my baby brother.

I've seen kids as little as four stick out their tongues and make evil little faces at him as though he wasn't even human. But Jimmy never gets angry. He doesn't beat them up or hate them forever. He just gives them a big old grin.

It's amazing to watch. First, his big, brown eyes grow sparkly, and the corners of his mouth begin to twitch. Then, when his smile does break, and his small, white teeth peek through those lips, it's as if the sun has broken through the clouds.

Some people say they feel sorry for Jimmy and that it's too bad he isn't "normal." But you know what? In a way, I wish everyone on this earth was like my brother. Because no matter how mean people are to him, he always has a smile.

So now, if people are mean to me or make fun of me, I just give them a big old grin, because I've learned from my little brother that it's not how much your brain has developed, or how many toes you have, it's how much your heart feels and how big a smile you wear.♥

UNCLE AL

Spencer Kagan

All things pass, but some things never change.

My first memory of Uncle Al is from a time before I actually met him. Mama Clara and "the rest" were talking about Sunny marrying a man "so much older." As I listened to them talk, I formed a strong mental image of Sunny—young, beautiful Sunny—about to marry someone older by far than Daddy Julie!

When I got to meet Uncle Al, I was shocked. He wasn't at all what I had imagined. He wore polo shirts, did back flips from a high dive, and took all the kids on motorcycle rides. He not only had his big motorcycle but lots of little motorbikes and scooters. He told me that when he took kids riding he felt like a mother duck with all her little ducks in a line behind her.

I was appointed ringbearer for the wedding. My job was easy. All I had to do was walk down the aisle holding a silk pillow with tassels. The pillow carried the most precious item of the wedding: the ring. I was instructed exactly how to hold the pillow, with both hands underneath, palms up. The ring was to be placed in the very center of my special silk pillow. I felt important. Proud. We practiced. I could handle this. I was honored to play such an important role in such a big event.

The day of the wedding arrived. Right before I was to walk down the aisle, two old ladies looked at me and started to discuss the possibility that the ring might fall off the pillow. I told them I'd be careful, but, as they continued to talk, I could feel a bit of uncertainty growing within me. Perhaps, one insisted, it *would* fall off. It *could* fall off. I didn't see how, but I had to admit to myself the possibility, and the more the old ladies discussed it, the more likely it seemed, even to me. I would be careful, I thought, but I could trip.

"We could pin the ring to the pillow," said one. I demurred. I would be careful. It would not be necessary.

The ladies ignored my protest. One of them reached under her dress and produced a small safety pin. Quickly she pinned the ring to the pillow. The other inspected the job. No, she concluded, the pin showed too much. They began to fuss with each other, arguing about who should pin the ring on the pillow.

I stood there, holding the pillow, hands underneath, palms up, while four hands on top of the pillow wrestled with the ring and the pin.

Finally, the second lady did the job. She managed to pin the ring from underneath so the pin barely showed. "Perfect," she declared as she straightened up, proudly surveying her work.

And just in time. It was time for me to walk down the aisle.

Feeling a bit of wind had been taken from my sail, I stood as straight as I could and mustered as much dignity as I could salvage. I could have made it without tripping, I thought as I walked—and without dropping the ring, even without their silly little safety pin.

I made my way to my assigned place, to the left and just behind Uncle Al. I waited. And waited. It seemed like forever until they got to the part where Uncle Al was to reach down and pick up the ring and place it on Aunt Sunny's finger.

Finally, the moment came. Uncle Al looked down, assured. There I was, with both hands under the pillow, doing my job, offering up the pillow, with the ring on top. Uncle Al reached down. He grasped the ring and began to lift it. And—to my horror—the pillow lifted with it.

I desperately wanted to tell him how the ring got attached to the pillow, that the pin wasn't my idea, but silence seemed the better course. So I just watched, helpless. Uncle Al's expression changed from assurance to dismay. He tried a second time to lift the ring. Again, the pillow came along with it.

I continued to watch Uncle Al's face. Dismay deepened, was replaced with a scowl. He bent to inspect the situation more closely. Now I could see his expression up close. A definite scowl. Then, under his breath, so low that only I could hear it, Uncle Al hissed: "Who the *hell* pinned the ring to the pillow?"

At that moment, I knew. I loved Uncle Al. And *that* has never changed.♥

THE WISDOM OF A CHILD

Richard E. Cunningham

The death of my mother was long and difficult. It took two years for the cancer to wear her away. I was teaching 200 miles from my parents' home but made frequent trips to do what I could to give emotional support to her and to my elderly father. At the end there were details to be taken care of—things my father had asked me to handle for him.

Finally it was over. The funeral had been that morning. Saddened friends and relatives had come and paid their respects and returned home. As I sat down at the kitchen table in my parents' house, my four-year-old son, John, looked up at me and said, "Daddy, let's play."

I tried to explain that I really didn't want to play, that I was very sad because Gramma had died. John replied, "I know that, Daddy. That's why you play, so you won't be sad. So you'll feel better."

We played. We went down to the pond and threw stones in the water. We made frogs jump.

We looked at the wild iris along the bank, and he was right. When we went back to the house, we did feel better.

One summer day nearly 30 years later, we lost John. It was an aneurysm, sudden and without warning. It was again the spirit of his childhood wisdom that helped us to go on, as it had so many years before.♥

THE SECRET OF A SUCCESSFUL MARRIAGE

Sherry Phelan

In eight years of married life, I've learned the secret of a successful marriage: Find a perfect husband and work hard to keep up with him.

This isn't easy to do when you're married to a man who not only finds pleasure in making the people in his life happy but does a great job of it. Nonetheless, I do my best.

Let me give you an example.

On a recent rainy Saturday when I needed to be away all day at a professional meeting, I conspired to make John's day special. He was still sleeping, so before I left I brought in the paper, made coffee, and put his favorite classical CDs on so they would greet him when he woke up. I tidied up the house (even the kitchen, a chore I'd rather avoid, especially early in the morning), lightly kissed him good-bye, and slipped out quietly, leaving a note that said, "I love you," on the seat of his car before I drove off.

The day was a tiring one, and when the meeting ended I faced an hour's drive home in stormy weather. All I could think of was chocolate chip cookies so, naturally, I stopped at a store. As I searched the aisles for the object of my desire, I remembered that John typically calls under similar circumstances to ask if there's anything we need. I headed for the phone.

"I'm at the store," I said, when John answered. "I stopped to get some chocolate chip cookies. Do we need anything else?"

"We have chocolate chip cookies," he responded. "I picked some up for you earlier." (Did I mention my husband is not only perfect, but psychic?)

As I pulled into the driveway, it was still pouring. Before I could get out of the car, John met me with an umbrella. He had also made the bed, usually *my* contribution. And to top it all off, he had arranged a special date night. He took me to an early movie, figuring I would need an absorbing diversion after an intense day, and then for an elegant dinner—one of my favorite treats.

I may never be able to match "the perfect husband," but I continue to try. And our marriage gets better and better.♥

BEFORE GRANDMAS MOVED TO FLORIDA AND UNCLES TO ARIZONA

Pat Wilson O'Leary

I grew up in Michigan during the 1950s, when family members lived close by. Both my mother and father worked full time, but I never spent a day in a day care center, and I wasn't left alone. My life was shaped not only by my parents and my older siblings but by two other relatives who raised and nurtured me: Grandma Wilson and Uncle Walt.

Annie Ludlam Wilson was a widow when I came along. She was unable to get out much, so she made herself available to serve my every need. My mother had problems with her back after my birth; she couldn't lift me out of the crib, so when my mother recovered and returned to work, I stayed at Grandma's.

Grandma and I spent days upon end together. We delighted in each other's company. I wasn't treated like a child; I was treated like a friend. We talked about many topics: the value of an education, religion, and the English royal family. We watched the relatively new miracle machine of television. We knitted. By the time I was five I could knit on four needles and do a myriad of stitches.

On the first day of kindergarten, I took my knitting bag to school, thinking we might have a break and I would have time to get in a few stitches. When "rug time" came, I took out my in-progress tea cozy and everyone laughed. They had never seen a kindergarten knitter! I was so embarrassed I put away the knitting, almost for good.

Grandma also taught me to serve meals in the style to which she was accustomed. She and Grandpa had owned a bed and breakfast inn on Morcombe Bay in the Lake District of England. Serving meals was her specialty. At her house, every meal required a tablecloth with cloth napkins. Sandwiches were served cut in triangles. Menu selections were made with both nutrition and color in mind. "People eat with their eyes," Grandma always said. Tea was served at 4 p.m., whether it was a fancy meat tea—like an early light dinner—or only buttered bread (triangles, of course). Cookies and cake were always served on a doilied plate. Flowers, fresh preferred, adorned the table. All the requirements came from Grandma's English background, from people who do things properly!

During first grade I stayed home more and didn't go to Grandma's as much. Uncle Walt— actually, my great-great uncle—was always there. He had come to live with us when I was six months old. He planned to stay only six months, but he lived in our house for 13 years and died when he was 92. Uncle Walt was my storyteller, my cook, my teacher, and my friend.

Walter Parrish came to the United States, via Canada, as a child, traveling alone from England. He educated himself and did apprentice work. He had made his living as a minstrel and gambler on the Mississippi riverboats, as a carpenter and master woodworker in New York state, and as a driver for touring cars in the West. His stories provided me with vicarious adventures from a time I'd never know.

Every school day I came home for lunch. Uncle Walt knew that I liked canned spaghetti and canned baked beans, so he took it upon himself to make a combination casserole. My older brother and sister stuck up their noses at it, but I loved it. I knew that dish had been made for me!

But the thing I remember most about Uncle Walt is his contribution to polishing my reading skills. His plan for self-improvement was based on the belief that "reading makes a difference in your life." When I was in the second grade I could read out loud, but without speed or grace. Weekly, Uncle Walt walked me to the library. Every day he and I read aloud, sitting on the grey couch in the living room or on the flowered lounge chair on our wide front porch. He gave me his time, his confidence, and his patience.

Grandma and Uncle Walt did not leave me a tangible inheritance, but what they did leave me is much more valuable. Along with the priceless gift of their love and attention, they each gave me a sense of family, history, and tradition.

Today my house is decorated like an English B & B. For family and company, I like to set a pretty table, use linen napkins and, of course, cut sandwiches into triangles. I am not only a voracious reader and an educator but a published author.

I am even thinking of taking up knitting again.♥

HIM

Josh Smothers
Age 14

I talk with him and see him every single day.
He may be a little impatient or annoying at times,
But that doesn't mean that I have to get mad,
You just have to bear with him and understand
    what he is going through.

He has cerebral palsy and is in a wheelchair,
But it doesn't mean that he is not like you or me.
He could very well lead a happier life than me
    even though he has this disease,
But it doesn't bother him in his eyes because he
    could care less about it!

When I am wheeling him in the mall or an
    unknown place to him,
People may stare and give me a dirty look,
But that doesn't phase me a bit,
Because these people don't understand the bond
    that we have, not even the beginning of it.

Some of the best doctors in Iowa said that he
    would never read, write, or talk,
But look at him now, he is learning how to walk.
He is a very outgoing and social person,
To him, everybody that wanted to could be his
    friend.

I try to do special things with him every single day,
When I go to bed at night I always pray.
We play games like Uno, Nintendo, Yatzee, and
    more,
He beats me all of the time and has wins galore!

His favorite color is yellow and cartoon is Barney.
Why is it Barney? I don't know,
But he can't miss even one of his shows.
If he wanted to, he could watch Barney or Disney
    movies 24 hours a day!

I hope you understand that I love him very much.
He is short, pudgy, has glasses, and a short-haired
    butch.
In the whole universe, there is NO other,
HE is Tyler and my loving brother!♥

A BRIDGE INTO SPRINGTIME

Mac Parker

My father died in the spring.

No, not recently. In fact, last year I was startled to realize that he had been gone for 27 years—exactly three-quarters of my lifetime.

I no longer have regrets. I have woven the experience of his death into the fabric of my life. At this point I feel genuinely grateful for the growth that his loss has required of me, and I can hardly imagine who I would be without this central and formative turning point.

Still, every year, as winter begins to loose its grip, I feel a certain dread. It is one of my life's most poignant paradoxes that spring—the season of new birth—is the time I most associate with death and grieving.

Thankfully, every spring, Jersey Drown is also part of the memory.

My father was sick for months before he died. There were many people who wanted to help, but few seemed capable of doing it. I was the youngest in my family, and perhaps our friends and neighbors felt too sad about my impending loss to allow them to come close enough to provide real comfort.

With Jersey it was different. For whatever reason, he found his way to me. I was only nine, and he had children of his own, but he made a point to call every weekend and invite me out into the woods of Vermont's "Northeast Kingdom," where we lived.

Jersey was—still is—a forester, and so, of course, a forester became what I wanted to be as well. Among other things, he taught me to walk on snowshoes as we cruised the woodlots under his care, marking boundaries and eating sandwiches toasted over an open fire.

I learned a lot from Jersey, but what I remember most is his reassuring presence at a time when the whole world seemed afraid of what was happening to me and to my family.

When the day finally came for my father to die, everyone knew, although none of us talked of it. My mother had the wisdom to send me up the hill to be with Jersey. We were outside when the phone call came. Jersey went in the house to take it, while I stayed by myself on the lawn. I remember sensing, perhaps even watching, my father leave, rising up into the skies over Lake Memphremagog. Young as I was, I felt as though I might even be pulled up with him.

Then Jersey was back beside me, his short, strong arm around my shoulders, and he told me simply that my father would not have to suffer anymore.

He may have cried. I know I did. Anchored by his presence, I grieved as a young boy should, feeling my loss with no danger of being lost myself.

As I have reached back over the years to process and heal whatever grief remains from my father's death, it is always Jersey I find standing there beside me. I've tried to tell him how much this means, but how can you express a gratitude so deep, so private? Yet, how can I not keep trying, especially in this season, when I feel it most?

Thank you, Jersey. You built me a sturdy bridge into springtime, and it is holding up well, even after all these years.♥

LESSONS IN BASEBALL

Chick Moorman

As an 11-year-old, I was addicted to baseball. I listened to baseball games on the radio. I watched them on TV. The books I read were about baseball. I took baseball cards to church in hopes of trading with other baseball card junkies. My fantasies? All about baseball.

I played baseball whenever and wherever I could. I played organized or sandlot. I played catch with my brother, with my father, with friends. If all else failed, I bounced a rubber ball off the porch stairs, imagining all kinds of wonderful things happening to me and my team.

It was with this attitude that I entered the 1956 Little League season. I was a shortstop. Not good, not bad. Just addicted.

Gordon was not addicted. Nor was he good. He moved into our neighborhood that year and signed up to play baseball. The kindest way of describing Gordon's baseball skills is to say that he didn't have any. He couldn't catch. He couldn't hit. He couldn't throw. He couldn't run.

In fact, Gordon was afraid of the ball.

I was relieved when the final selections were made and Gordon was assigned to another team. Everyone had to play at least half of each game, and I couldn't see Gordon improving my team's chances in any way. Too bad for the other team.

After two weeks of practice, Gordon dropped out. My friends on his team laughed when they told me how their coach directed two of the team's better players to walk Gordon into the woods and have a chat with him. "Get lost" was the message that was delivered, and "get lost" was the one that was heard.

Gordon got lost.

That scenario violated my 11-year-old sense of justice, so I did what any indignant shortstop would do. I tattled. I told my coach the whole story. I shared the episode in full detail, figuring my coach would complain to the League office and have Gordon returned to his original team. Justice and my team's chances of winning would both be served.

I was wrong. My coach decided that Gordon needed to be on a team that wanted him—one that treated him with respect, one that gave everyone a fair chance to contribute according to their own ability.

Gordon became my team member.

I wish I could say Gordon got the big hit in the big game with two outs in the final inning. It didn't happen. I don't think Gordon even hit a foul ball the entire season. Baseballs hit in his direction (right field) went over him, by him, through him, or off him.

It wasn't that Gordon didn't get help. The coach gave him extra batting practice and worked with him on his fielding, all without much improvement.

I'm not sure if Gordon learned anything from my coach that year. I know I did. I learned to bunt without tipping off my intention. I learned to tag up on a fly if there were less than two outs. I learned to make a smoother pivot around second base on a double play.

I learned a lot from my coach that summer, but my most important lessons weren't about baseball. They were about character and integrity. I learned that everyone has worth, whether they can hit .300 or .030. I learned that we all have value, whether we can stop the ball or have to turn and chase it. I learned that doing what is right, fair, and honorable is more important than winning or losing.

It felt good to be on that team that year. I'm grateful that man was my coach. I was proud to be his shortstop and his son.♥

MORE *WHERE THE HEART IS?*

All of the vignettes, poems, and stories in this book were sent to us by people who believed so strongly in the importance of family they were willing to share their ideas with others. After an initial mailed request to professional speakers, educators, friends, and family, stories began to arrive daily. The response was quick and massive. We received over 300 submissions in a 60 day period, which confirmed our belief that love of home and family is clearly an issue that touches people and moves them to action.

Now you can help. I am planning to publish at least two more volumes—*Where the Heart Is: More Stories of Home and Family* and *Where the Heart Is: 365 Days a Year*. Please send me articles, vignettes, poems, stories, or helpful parenting tips that you'd like to share. I'm looking for contributions that

1. promote family solidarity;

2. tell what is good and noble about parenting;

3. communicate the warmth and dignity of positive family relationships;

4. touch the soul; or

5. communicate the importance and responsibility inherent in parenting.

It is time to show the world models of parenting that nurture, uplift, inspire, and communicate mutual respect among all family members. Help me celebrate family strength, love, hope, and commitment through your written contributions. Send them to:

Chick Moorman
Personal Power Press
P.O. Box 5985
Saginaw, MI 48603
Fax: (517)791-6711

If your contribution is selected for publication, a biographical sketch, photo, and information on how readers can contact you will be included, if you choose.

PASS IT ON

Many people have helped me make the dream of this book come true. In addition to the story contributors, numerous others have read, typed, suggested, inspired, rated, and reacted to the material in *Where the Heart Is*. There is no way I can possibly repay them.

People helped me with this book because they believe in its main message: *Home and family are important.* They helped because they know that every child in every family has value. They helped because they realize the best way to change the world is one family at a time. I am deeply indebted to them all.

I subscribe to the old adage, "Don't repay a kindness; pass it on." Getting this book and the material it contains into as many hands and hearts as possible is the best way I know of to honor the people who have contributed to it.

Please help me share these stories and practical parenting strategies with others. Give your copy of

Where the Heart Is to a friend. Pass it around your neighborhood. Buy one for Uncle Joe's birthday. Tell your minister, your babysitter, your line dance teacher about the ideas contained in its pages. Give it to someone you love. Help us to help families.

Pass it on.

FURTHER TRAINING TO IMPROVE YOUR SKILLS

OPTION 1

Send for information about the *Where the Heart Is Workshop Kit*. The kit consists of discussion topics, parent workbooks, suggested activities, homework assignments, and a facilitator guide— everything you need to run a ten-session workshop to promote family solidarity.

OPTION 2

Send for information about how to arrange a one- or two-day parent training by Chick Moorman in your location. You will receive information on how to set up a training, find a site, build attendance, and do follow-up.

Write the Institute for Personal Power, P.O. Box 5985, Saginaw, MI 48603 or call 517/791-3533.

OTHER BOOKS BY CHICK MOORMAN

TALK SENSE TO YOURSELF: THE LANGUAGE OF PERSONAL POWER

by Chick Moorman (paperback) $12.95

There is a connection between the words you use, the beliefs you hold, and the actions you take. This book explores that connection and shows you how you can purposefully select language that creates within you the programming necessary to change the quality and direction of your life.

Contained within the book is a series of words, phrases and ways of speaking that will increase your sense of personal power. *TALK SENSE TO YOURSELF: The Language of Personal Power* will help you structure your language patterns to put more choice and possibility in your life. You will become more self-confident, improve your self-esteem, and learn how to talk sense to yourself.

OUR CLASSROOM: WE CAN LEARN TOGETHER

by Chick Moorman and Dee Dishon (hard cover) $19.95

This book will help K-6 teachers create a classroom environment where discipline problems are less likely to occur, and where students are less likely to activate the new three R's — Resistance, Reluctance, and Resentment. It will show you how to build an atmosphere of togetherness and cooperation, and focuses on activities and strategies that foster notions of belonging, interdependence and mutual respect.

TEACHER TALK: WHAT IT REALLY MEANS

by Chick Moorman and Nancy Moorman/Weber (paperback) $12.95

This book is about teachers' talk — the comments, questions, commands, and suggestions that teachers direct at students every day. It explores the way teachers talk to children and exposes the underlying "silent messages" that accompany their spoken words.

Eighty percent of all talking in classrooms is done by teachers. Sometimes that talk is lecture. Other times it involves giving directions, reprimanding, reminding, praising, suggesting, discussing, motivating, or explaining. Regardless of its form, teacher talk makes up eighty percent of classroom talk.

Your choice of words and your language selections are critical to the self-esteem, the academic success, and the healthy mental and emotional development of your students. There is an undeniable link between the words you speak and the attitudes and outcomes students create in their lives. By selecting words and phrases *intentionally*; by altering your present language; by adding to or taking away from your common utterances you can empower your students and enhance their learning. *TEACHER TALK: What It Really Means* will help you to do just that.

To order any of these books, call (517) 791-3533 or send the order form below to Personal Power Press, Box 5985, Saginaw, MI 48603.

BOOK ORDER FORM

	Price	Qty.	Total
Where The Heart Is (paperback)	$14.95		
Talk Sense To Yourself (paperback)	$12.95		
Our Classroom: We Can Learn Together (hard cover)	$19.95		
Teacher Talk: What It Really Means (paperback)	$12.95		
MI residents add 6% sales tax			
Shipping & handling			
Total			

Name: _____

Address: _____

City: _____ State _____ Zip _____

Phone Number: _____

Please add the following shipping and handling charges:

$0-$15.00 . . . . $3.75
$15.01-$30.00 . . . . $4.75
$30.01-$50.00 . . . . $5.75
$50.01 and up . . . . $10% of total order
Canada: 20% of total order. US funds only, please.

CONTRIBUTORS

Debra Zagorsky Agliano is an active realtor and speaker in greater Boston. Her mission statement sums up her attitude: "I believe that each person I come in contact with in my life is a unique individual and deserves to be treated as such. Each person, each situation, and each home will be treated with enthusiasm, creativity, and sensitivity." She shares her life with her husband, Frank. Contact Debra at ERA Andrew Realty, 12 High Street, Medford, MA 02155, (617)395-7676.

Lisa Albrecht has grown up since she wrote the poem about her grandfather. She has been with American Airlines for the last five and one-half years working as a flight attendant. Lisa is also an independent distributor for The Peoples Network, a company truly making a difference in our society by putting values back in homes across North America and Canada. This foundation is dedicated to helping people receive positive, helpful information on an ongoing basis that unfortunately has never before been available. Lisa can be reached at 1857 Bennett Place, Des Plaines, IL 60018 or by telephone at (708)586-5661.

Mitch Anthony is an award-winning author (*Campus Life Book of the Year - '92*) of two books for and about teens. He is a nationally-recognized speaker to youth and to educators with a decade of experience in 1000+ schools. He hosts a syndicated radio show, *The Daily Dose,* heard on stations throughout America. Mitch is the developer of educational programs on *Conflict Resolution, Peer Mediation, Peer Helping, Teen Sexuality* and other youth concerns which are being used in hundreds of schools across the United States and in other countries around the world. He is the founder and developer of the National Suicide Education Center and 12 youth-oriented public service organizations. You can contact him at (507)282-2723.

Mary Montle Bacon earned a B.A. from Fordham University, majoring in Spanish and French. Graduate education was at Stanford University, where she earned an M.A. in guidance and counseling and a Ph.D. in social psychology. An experienced teacher, university instructor, counselor, psychologist, and administrator, Dr. Bacon is currently a full-time consultant sharing her services throughout the country. Sample presentation topics include "Trends, Like Horses, Are Easier to Ride in the Direction They Are Going . . . "; No Malice Required: The Challenge of Diversity Viewing the World from Multiple Perspectives"; "Them That Gots the Gold, Makes the Rules: Empowering the Challenged Client." Contact her at 1055 Lakeview Drive, Hillsborough, CA 94010, (415)342-0621, fax (415)347-6011.

Patricia Ball, CSP, CPAE, is president of Corporate Communications, vice-president of the National Speakers Association (NSA), a Certified Speaking Professional, Communications Specialist, Keynoter, and Diversity Trainer. Since 1972, she has helped thousands of executives, salespeople, and others achieve greater success in their personal and professional lives. Patricia is currently president elect of NSA and in July 1996 will be president. Her superb talent for customizing programs to meet organizational needs has become her recognized trademark. Patricia is listed in the *World Who's Who of Women,* and her book *Straight Talk Is More Than Words* will be published by year end 1995. Contact Patricia at Corporate Communications, 9875 Northbridge Road, St. Louis, MO 63124, (314)966-5452.

Dr. Richard Benedict is currently a high school principal at L'Anse Creuse High School in Mt. Clemens, Michigan. He's been a teacher, coach, counselor, alternative educator, university lecturer, educational consultant, and director of Enterprise Programs. In addition to his administrative role at L'Anse Creuse High School, Rick is director of Educational Decisionmaking Services, a firm dedicated to helping parents, teachers, schools, and students make good decisions about educational programming. If you'd like to read the book, *Trash Can Kids*, write Rick at Educational Decisionmaking Services, 35531 Stillmeadow Lane, Suite 531, Clinton Township, MI 48035.

Dr. Jane Bluestein is a dynamic and entertaining personality who has trained thousands of educators, counselors, and parents worldwide, appearing internationally as a speaker and talk-show guest to discuss issues such as self-esteem, discipline, motivation, achievement, prevention, boundary-setting, and the secrets of positive mentorship. Formerly a classroom teacher and crisis-intervention counselor, Dr. Bluestein is the author of *21st Century Discipline, Being a Successful Teacher, Parents in a Pressure Cooker, Parents, Teens, & Boundaries*, and her latest, *Mentors, Masters, and Mrs. McGregor: Stories of Teachers Making a Difference.* Jane currently serves as the president of Instructional Support Services, Inc., a consulting and resource firm in Albuquerque, New Mexico. (160 Washington SE, Suite 64, Albuquerque, NM 87108, 1-800-688-1960, (505)255-3007, fax (505)255-3098).

Ann Brewster, M.A., director of <u>Ann Brewster Associates,</u> has dedicated herself to the development and improvement of human relationships. An educator, Ann recognized early in her career that one's successes in most endeavors depend upon the ability to communicate and to effectively manage relationships with others. A skilled presenter with 15 years of experience, she has conducted seminars, workshops, and individual consultations with the education, business, and service communities. Her programs include communications skills, team building, and stress management. Clients describe her presentation manner as confident, competent, and caring. Ann's story, "First Day of School," is from a series of books called *Family Ties* dedicated to communication between generations. She can be reached at 286 Stone Rd., Fremont, MI 49412. Ph/fax (616)924-2488.

Mike Buettell has dedicated the last 23 years of his life to the growth and development of young adolescents as a junior high teacher and school counselor. His award-winning plays, "The Haunted Mansion," "Greatest Little Show on Earth," and "Hillbilly Cafe," are available, free of charge, to any interested junior high drama department. In his spare time, he can be found exploring the remote areas of the world as an adventurer and world class mountaineer. He can be reached in care of Rancho Middle School, 4861 Michelson, Irvine, CA 92715.

Ben Burton is a full-time professional speaker and writer residing in Hot Springs, Arkansas. The Burton family—Ben, his wife LaVerne, daughters Boni and Bev, and sons Bruce and Brooks—were named Arkansas' All-American Family in 1971 and competed in the national finals in Florida. As hobbies and special interests, Burton lists fishing, running, beekeeping, music and writing. Most of the stories included here are excerpted from Ben's first book, *The Chicken That Won a Dogfight.* The book is available by mail—paperback or hardcover with a free program tape—by calling 1-800-833-2148. Ben, a humorist with inspiration and songs, speaks approximately 70 times per year and can be reached to discuss booking at 10 Queens Row, Hot Springs, AR 71901, (501)623-6496.

Leo Buscaglia has a Ph.D. from the University of Southern California. He is an educator, not a psychologist. Over 11,000,000 copies of his books have been sold. *Love; Living, Loving and Learning;* and *Loving Each Other* have sold over a million copies each. Editions of Dr. Buscaglia's books are available in 19 languages, in 24 editions. One of his books, *The Fall of Freddie the Leaf,* has been adapted to audio cassette, educational film and a one-hour ballet. Leo Buscaglia's *Love Cookbook with Biba Caggiano* is his newest release. It was published in fall, 1994. Dr. Buscaglia was one of the first ten inductees in the Hershey's Hugs Hall of Fame in 1993. He is the Chairman of the Felice (Fee-LEE-Chay) Foundation, which is dedicated to encouraging and teaching the spirit of giving in our society.

Karyn Buxman hails from Hannibal, Missouri—home of the other great humorist, Mark Twain. A leading national expert on therapeutic humor, Karyn has put her humor studies to work through speaking, writing, and consulting. She's editor for the American Association for Therapeutic Humor and vice-president of *The Journal of Nursing Jocularity,* a national humor magazine for nurses, and has produced numerous audio and video tapes. She's also a member of the National Speakers Association. Coming from a health care background, Karyn Buxman now works full time as a speaker and author, sharing with audiences across the nation the benefits of therapeutic humor. To see how your group can benefit from some "mirth aid," contact Karyn at P.O. Box 1273, Hannibal, MO 63401-1273 or call 1-800-848-6679.

Rick Carson. When it comes to gremlin taming, Rick Carson wrote the book—literally. He is the author of several publications, including two Harper Collins books, *Taming Your Gremlin* and *Never Get a Tattoo. Taming Your Gremlin* has been on the stand for 10 years and is included in Harper's prestigious Perennial Library. It is available not only in English, but in Japanese and Portuguese as well. Rick is also featured on several Nightingale-Conant cassette series, including the *Inner Awakening Library* featuring Rick, Dr. Deepak Chopra, and others. In his Dallas-based offices, Rick and his staff assist individuals, families, businesses, and professional associations with tough transitions, rough relationships, and organizational snags. He can be reached at 1-800-253-9269.

Gerald Coffee, considered one of the nation's top speakers, addresses many prestigious business and leadership groups each year. Born in Modesto, California, he joined the Navy in 1958 after graduating from UCLA with a major in business administration. He served his country as a Naval officer for 28 years, seven of them as a prisoner of war in the communist prisons of North Vietnam. After returning from Vietnam, he received his master's degree in political science and then attended the esteemed National Defense University in Washington, D.C. Captain Coffee has earned many military awards and decorations, including the Silver Star, as well as numerous civilian awards. Retired from the Navy since 1985, he now lives in Hawaii. To engage Captain Coffee as a speaker or to order copies of *Beyond Survival* (book/audio/video), call 1-800-840-1776.

Dave Cowles is a practicing psychotherapist and addictions counselor. He is presently the Clinical Supervisor for Ten-Sixteen Home of Midland, Michigan. At age 52, divorced, and with a son and daughter both grown, he is enjoying middle age in the company of his roommate and co-pilot, Tori. Tori, by the way, is a mixed lab/golden retriever who goes everywhere with him. He spends his free(?) time writing, playing music, not catching fish, and enjoying the wilderness. You can contact him at 4851 Wilson Drive, Gladwin, MI 48624.

Richard E. Cunningham holds a Ph.D. in education. He is a veteran of 28 years in the classroom with teaching experience in art, sociology, psychology, and graduate courses in education. With colleague Lynne Zimmer he has given workshops and presentations in learned helplessness, learning styles, and classroom management for new teachers. He is a supervisor of student teachers in their classroom assignments. His current project is research on the relationships of experience, learning, and the mind. Dick lives in northern Michigan with his wife, Nancy. He can be reached at 622 W. Michigan Ave., Boyne City, MI 49712, (616)582-9373.

Randi Curtiss is a 14-year-old high school freshman from Alliance, Nebraska. Although born in Lincoln, she has spent all but six months of her life in the Nebraska panhandle. As the oldest of six children, she resides on a patch of native prairie grass with her parents, one brother, and four sisters. Her writing is a reflection of the land she lives in and the people and animals who inhabit it. She can be contacted at P.O. Box 460, Alliance, NE 69301.

Stan Dale, formerly the voice of "The Shadow" and the announcer/narrator of "The Lone Ranger," "Sgt. Preston" and "The Green Hornet" radio shows, is the Director/Founder of the Human Awareness Institute in San Mateo, California. He conducts "Sex, Love and Intimacy Workshops" around the world. Stan is the author of *Fantasies Can Set You Free* and *My Child, My Self: How to Raise the Child You Always Wanted to Be.* Both books are available from The Human Awareness Institute, 1720 S. Amphlett Blvd., Suite 128, San Mateo, CA 94402. Call 1-800-800-4117 or (415)571-5524.

Sandra Darling is currently working for New Hampshire Technical College/ Nashua, Division of Community Education, where she finds it a pleasure being part of a team servicing people who are furthering their education. With her unique writing style, she's just beginning to develop her talent. Drawing from real life experiences enables her to write numerous short stories. Sandra is presently looking for an interested publishing house where three books titled "Postcard Perfect," "The Final Draw," and "Destination" can surface in readers' homes to enjoy. Future writing goal: having readers enjoy her storytelling and relate to the characters as they unfold. She would be happy to hear from anyone interested in reading, promoting, or publishing her writings. Contact her at 7 Pierce Street, Nashua, NH 03060.

Kenneth G. Davis is a board-certified family physician and addictionologist who has practiced in Conroe, Texas, since 1978. He and his wife Kitty have two daughters in college. He is an avid cyclist and writes and speaks on the topic of cycling as a metaphor for life ("Keeping Your Balance and Shifting Gears"). Contact him at 1915 N. Frazier St., Conroe, TX 77301, (409)756-3321

Bill Decker has taught, modeled, and coached self-esteem building and communication skills for 20 years. He has worked with parents and teachers on classroom and family strategies. Bill's current focus is the business community. He believes that if you go beyond corporate buzz words the bedrock foundation of productive and satisfying working relationships is clarity, dialogue, and mutual respect. He has taught the skills to achieve this to all levels of the corporate structure. Bill can be reached at 421 S. Clinton St., Oak Park, IL 60302, (708)383-1170; whdthree@aol.com.

Dr. Joachim de Posada has studied psychological techniques that enhance human performance for over 20 years. He uses self-hypnosis and visualization methods to help individuals explore the deepest parts of the subconscious, recognize and eliminate mental barriers, and dramatically improve competitive performance. Dr. de Posada is a consultant to Fortune 500 corporations, professional and Olympic teams, and individual athletes. Dr. de Posada is considered by many to be one of the world's top trainers in sales, motivation, management and customer service and Total Quality Management. He designed and implemented the University of Miami's Sales Institute in the School of Continuing Studies, teaching Psychology Applied to Sales, Management and Negotiation Skills. Presently he is an adjunct professor and lecturer at the University. Contact him at 1111 S.W. 92nd Ave., Miami, FL 33174, (305)889-4689, (800)723-9165 ext. 865, fax (305)220-6524.

Kenneth R. Freeston, Ph.D., is the superintendent of schools for Easton and Redding, Connecticut. His articles on education and parenting have been published in the *New York Times, Education Week* and *Educational Leadership.* He is a frequent radio and television talk show guest and often consults with school systems and professional education groups on school improvement and quality management. He is the co-author of *Welcome to Club Dad: Mostly True Reflections on Fatherhood* (Meadowbrook, 1994), a collection of essays on the child in the man. If you look in his kitchen carefully, you can see the place where wishbones wait. Contact him at Boards of Education, 215 Center Road, Easton, CT 06612, (203)261-2513, fax (203)261-4549.

Dr. Ed Frierson is an award-winning educator and one of the premier speakers in America today. His presentations are notable for their timely ideas and for their uplifting spirit. Dr. Ed's keynotes and seminars help you bring out the best in yourself and all those in your organization regardless of differences in background or abilities. Ed brings extraordinary practical experience to the audience. He is the father of six children including TWO SETS OF TWINS! Dr. Ed's newest seminar, *Building Learning Communities*, is now available on video. To get information or to arrange a speaking event with Dr. Ed "live," contact: Teaching For The 21st Century, 1-800-497-2001.

Shirley D. Garrett is a full-time professional speaker who uses humor and magic for an unforgettable impact on her audiences. Shirley' s quick wit and contagious laugh create an atmosphere for personal and professional growth. Surviving some of life's tougher lessons, Shirley speaks from the heart, using her experience to create magical moments in the lives of others. With a Doctorate of Education, Shirley brings expertise and experience to corporations, associations, and educational communities. Shirley takes her work seriously and herself lightly as she delivers keynote addresses, workshops, and retreats. Her most requested topics include: *It's a Full Time Job Just Being Me!; Handling Stress with Humor!; It's a Juggle Out There!; Change . . . Opportunity ISNOWHERE!;* and *Connecting During Conflict.* Shirley can be reached at (770)836-1926 or by writing Post Office Box 1195, Carrollton, GA 30117.

Oliver Gaspirtz was born November 20, 1970, in Aachen, West Germany. He moved to New York and married his wife Debbie in February of 1993. Oliver worked for a small Manhattan newspaper as cartoonist and art director until his first book, "The Truth About Cinderella," was published in December of 1993. His award-winning cartoons frequently appear in many magazines, including *The Weekly Farce, Funny Times, Sun, Cartoon Comedy Club, Snickers, Satire, Slugfest,* and *Police Beat.* His cartoons have also appeared in the two KFS series "The New Breed" and "Laf-A-Day." In Germany, Oliver's feature "Schwarzer Humor" appears once a week in several hundred papers. He can be reached at 9114 Avenue N, Brooklyn, NY, USA 11236, (718)209-1454.

Jessica Hill is a recent graduate of Brockport College, where she studied creative writing and photography. Under the guidance and urgings of her professors and friends, she's concentrating on her current project, inspired by her family and the experiences they shared on her grandparents' farm in Cattaraugus, New York. She's struggling to recapture those subtle mysteries of youth and to understand how they affect her life now, as an adult. She dedicates this project to her late grandmother, Clara Alberta Peters-Pepperdine, who was the real storyteller of her family. Jessica has three poems being published in *A Book of Their Own.* She is currently living with her parents and is receptive to any comments or advice readers are willing to offer. Contact her at 5800 Pittsford-Palmyra Road, Pittsford, NY 14534.

Diane Dickie Hodges, Ph.D., is an educator and a dynamic, motivational, insightful speaker. She is the Human Resources Director for a large school district and travels internationally giving presentations. Her areas of focus are self-esteem in the workplace, developing professional and student portfolios, adult life cycle changes, and employee appreciation and recognition. In all her presentations she incorporates the need to maintain a sense of humor. She has been an elementary school counselor, a secondary and central office administrator, and an instructor and administrator at the community college and university levels. She has received numerous state and national awards for educational leadership. She may be reached by contacting Threshold Presentations, 7786 St. Andrews Circle, Kalamazoo, MI 49002, (616)324-5272 or (616)674-8091.

D. Trinidad Hunt has been called a visionary with an inspiring message for people of all ages. As an international award-winning author, keynote speaker, corporate trainer, and business consultant, she combines skill training with humor and storytelling in a rare and magical way. Her works include: *Learning to Learn — Maximizing Your Performance Potential* (book and book on tape plus supplemental music and centering tapes to enhance learning) and *Remember to Remember Who You Are*, a small gift book of poetry. Trin's newest book, *The Operator's Manual for Planet Earth*, will be released in hardback by Hyperion Publishing Company in March of 1996. Call or fax for products and other information. 1-800-707-3526 or fax (808)239-2482.

Avril Johannes was born in England. She has three grown children, is a professional aviculturist, and has published short stories in *Bird Breeder, Alaska Magazine*, various newspapers, and *A 2nd Helping of Chicken Soup for the Soul*. She is currently working on a book about Alaska, where she lived for 20 years. Avril may be reached at 8070 New Hope Road, Grants Pass, OR 97527.

Dr. Spencer Kagan received his doctorate from UCLA in clinical psychology, with minors in social and developmental psychology. For 17 years he was a professor in the University of California publishing over 60 scientific books, book chapters, and journal articles, focusing on the development of cooperation. In 1990 Dr. Kagan established Kagan Cooperative Learning, a company dedicated to improving education by developing and distributing workshops, training institutes, books and teaching resources for cooperative learning. Kagan Cooperative Learning is the world's largest distributor of cooperative learning books and training seminars. Dr. Kagan is sought internationally as a speaker and workshop presenter. He may be reached at Kagan Cooperative Learning, 27134 Paseo Espada, Suite 303, San Juan Capistrano, CA 92675, 1(800)COOP LRN.

Amy Beth Kavanaugh is 14 years old. She was born on September 25, 1980, in Nashua, New Hampshire. Her sign is Libra, meaning balance. She is a freshman at Thurston High School. Amy enjoys writing poetry, listening to all kinds of music, drawing, basketball, and zodiacal signs. Her favorite basketball team is the Phoenix Suns, favorite colors are all shades of purple, and favorite Disney movie is *Beauty and the Beast*. Special awards that she's received include two second place medals for choir at a District Choral Festival for M.V.S.A., Judge's Choice Award, and a first place trophy at Cedar Point in eighth grade at Pierce Middle School. You can contact her at 15650 Norwich, Livonia, MI 48154.

Joe Kogel was already a national award-winning writer when, at age 25, he received a diagnosis of cancer. It woke him up. Now he wakes others up with an inspirational talk that is real and riveting and very, very funny. He has spoken nationally for 11 years, including appearances on MBC, CNN, and National Public Radio. Joe's audiences are all touched with the understanding that inside the great difficulties in life often lie the greatest gifts. His own book is due out soon. For information about his presentation, videotapes, and upcoming book, call (401)351-0229 or write 50 Summit Avenue, Providence, RI 02906.

MaryAnn Faubion Kohl, owner of Bright Ring Publishing, is the author of creative art idea books for children and the adults who care for them. Her interest in creative art for children comes from years of teaching elementary and preschool children and raising her own daughters. MaryAnn's books include these award-winning titles: *Scribble Cookies: Creative Independent Art Experiences for Children; Good Earth Art: Environmental Art for Kids; Science Arts: Discovering Science Through Art Experiences; Preschool Art: It's the Process Not the Product; Cooking Art: Experiencing Art in Cooking for Young Children.* MaryAnn also works as an educational consultant in art, illustrating, and publishing for young authors. She enjoys being with her family, reading, playing with her computer, and boating in the islands. MaryAnn can be reached at P.O. Box 31338, Bellingham, WA 98228, (360)734-1601.

Jim Lamancusa, a bright and clever 16-year-old, has a quick wit and personal charm which bring about an instant attraction. At 13 Jim wrote his first book. At 15 he became a professional speaker, motivating children, teachers, and parents to reach their goals and establish better communications. Jim has been a columnist in two magazines, appears on television, and is very active in athletics as well as leadership activities at Hoover High School. He lettered in diving and track in the ninth grade and is involved in soccer and cross-country. As a freshman he placed tenth in the state on the Hoover Speech Team. Write or call for more information on seminars and presentations: Lamancusa Live! Jim Lamancusa, P.O. Box 2717#PPP, North Canton, OH 44720, (216)494-7224, fax (216)494-2918.

Joe Lamancusa is a powerful professional speaker who travels nationally and internationally each year helping small business owners in the creative industries prosper and grow within the current business environment. His *Power Series* of seminars includes Customer Service, Advertising, Display, and Balancing Work and Family. Joe is the business editor of the FLORALTRENDS section in *CRAFTRENDS* magazine. He is the executive producer for the popular PBS show *Kathy Lamancusa's at Home with Flowers*. Joe is the president of Visual Design Concepts, a marketing, advertising, and consulting company within the creative industries. Write or call for more information on seminars, presentations, books and videos to: Lamancusa Live! Joe Lamancusa, P.O. Box 2717#PPP, North Canton, OH 44720, (216)494-7224, fax (216)494-2918.

Joe Lamancusa Jr. at age 18 has accomplished an incredible amount in his young life. He wrote his first book at 14, was a columnist in two magazines, has done numerous radio programs, and can regularly be seen on cable and network television. His book, *Kid Cash, Creative Money Making Ideas*, was reviewed in the business section of the *Wall Street Journal*. He is involved in numerous leadership activities and is captain of the varsity volleyball team at Hoover High School. Joe is an exciting professional speaker who motivates children, teachers, and parents to set and reach goals. Write or call for more information on seminars and presentations: Lamancusa Live! Joe Lamancusa Jr., P.O. Box 2717#PPP, North Canton, OH 44720, (216)494-7224, fax (216)494-2918.

Kathy Lamancusa, CPD, CCD, MSF, is a dynamic professional speaker, author, and television personality. She travels nationally and internationally each year, creatively touching the lives of her audiences. Her topics include Family Lifestyle, Creativity and Creative Skills. Over 1 million copies of Kathy's books and videos have been sold throughout the world. She will motivate, inspire, educate, and delight the members of any audience. Kathy has a column in several national and international consumer magazines. Her show *Kathy Lamancusa's at Home with Flowers* appears on PBS stations around the country. Kathy creates programs designed for general audiences, parents, teachers, and students. Write or call for more information on seminars, presentations, books and videos to: Lamancusa Live! Kathy Lamancusa, P.O. Box 2717#PPP, North Canton, OH 44720, (216)494-7224, fax (216)494-2918.

Sharon Lambert finds life challenging and fulfilling as a teacher of second graders at East Elementary USD 427 in Belleville, Kansas. Throughout the years, she has brought her message of faith, family, and encouragement to women's groups and Sunday morning worship services. Sharon often commutes between her home in Belleville and her hometown of Smith Center. She is active in her churches in both places, and during the summer she teaches the young adult class in the old country church founded by her ancestors. She can be reached at 801 17th Street, Belleville, KS 66935.

Nancy Crouch Lewis, M.Ed., has had a lifelong love affair with words. She began her professional career as an English teacher in Connecticut. Although she left both teaching and New England over 30 years ago, her love for and fascination with the English language have persisted and been reflected in subsequent activities as a writer, a librarian, and a facilitator/editor for people compiling their life stories. She currently lives in Little Rock, Arkansas, where she and her husband own and run Wellpower, Inc., a health education consulting firm. Nancy can be reached about her writing/editorial services by mail at 6818 Archwood Dr., Little Rock, AR 72204 or by phone at (501)562-3027 or (501)565-8144.

Miles L. McCall, Ph.D., is an innovative consultant, speaker, and author. Each year he has the opportunity to speak and consult with over 15,000 people. From rollerblading into the annual meeting of stockholders to standing atop a 12-foot ladder, Miles has an incredible ability to mix life and leadership into a new "art" form called learning. His current book, *Living Leadership: The Power of a Professional Parent*, is a collection of life lessons that inspire parents to be more professional at home. Miles is becoming known as the father of THM (Take Home Management), a unique approach to applying corporate training and development lessons on the home front. It's good for companies, it's good for employees, it's good for the family . . . which means it's good for our future! Contact: Dr. Miles McCall at Holly Oaks Farm, Rt 8, Box 3790, Hwy 21 West, Nacogdoches, TX 75964, Phone: (409)569-4790, fax (409)569-6844.

Chick Moorman has decided to become a cowboy. He loves Arabian horses, drives a truck, and is an adept country dancer. He knows how to do the Tush Push, Side Kick, Wooden Nickel, Blue Rose, Waltz, 2-Step, Swing, '50s Bop, T-R-O-U-B-L-E, Cowboy Cha Cha, El Paso, Desperado Wrap, Schottische, Walkin' Wazzi, and over 100 other country dances. In addition, he displays excellent dance floor etiquette. To invite him to your country dance club or to speak to your parent or teacher group, write the Institute For Personal Power, P.O. Box 5985, Saginaw, MI 48603 or call (517)791-3533, fax (517)791-6711.

Jenny Moorman currently lives in Vero Beach, Florida, where she spends her time as the primary caregiver for her grandfather. She believes it is essential to aid our loved ones in their transition from this lifetime. She is a former Peace Corps volunteer, having lived and worked in a rural community in Senegal, West Africa. Jenny is a graduate of Western Michigan University. You can contact her c/o Neltje Brauer, 3728 WindingWay, Kalamazoo, MI 49004.

Young Jay Mulkey, Ph.D., has been the president of the Character Education Institute for the last 13 years. Dr. Mulkey received his B.S. in education from Texas Christian University, an M.Ed. in administration and supervision from Our Lady of the Lake University, and a Ph.D. in curriculum and instruction from the University of Texas at Austin. One of the originators of the Character Education Curriculum 26 years ago, Dr. Mulkey has dedicated his life to developing responsible citizens. He spent 17 years as an elementary school teacher, 3 years as an art instructor, and 23 years as an instructor of Adult Basic Education. Dr. Mulkey enjoys reading, collecting and refinishing antiques, and playing bridge. Contact him at the Character Education Institute, 8918 Tesoro Dr., Suite 575, San Antonio, TX 78217, 1-800-284-0499.

Kim Namenye is 11 years old and going into the seventh grade at Davison Middle School in Davison, Michigan. She lives with her two sisters and mom and dad. She likes to write and she enjoys reading. Kim is on the seventh-grade cheerleading squad. She just returned from cheerleading camp and is really excited about going back to school! Her sixth-grade English teacher inspired her to write this poem.

Fran O'Connell is an educational consultant for a national training and development company and teaches off-campus graduate courses for Marygrove College. She designs and delivers customized training programs to meet a variety of personal and professional development needs. Fran offers workshops throughout Michigan, bringing a fresh, humorous perspective to the life challenges that face us all. Popular topics include "Family Matters: Making Moments Count," "HUMP (Having Umpteen Million Priorities)," "Spiritual Development of Children," and "It's Hard to Be the Grown-Up When You Live with a Bunch of Kids" (a workshop for parents with three or more children). Fran lives in a suburb of Detroit with her husband and four children. You can contact her at 29660 Rutherland, Southfield, MI 48076, (810)569-8729.

Pat Wilson O'Leary is a wife and mother. She is also a public speaker in the area of cooperative learning and teambuilding. Pat has presented her skill-building seminars to thousands of educators across the United States, Canada, and Puerto Rico. She is co-author, with Dee Dishon, of *A Guidebook for Cooperative Learning*, Learning Publications, Inc., Holmes Beach, FL (2nd edition, 1994). Pat can be contacted at Educational Excellence, 7703 Primrose Lane, Kalamazoo, MI 49002, phone/fax (616)327-2199.

Mac Parker has been making his living as a storyteller since 1988. He has performed widely around the U.S., including featured appearances at the National Folk Festival and the National Storytelling Festival. He has produced three storytelling cassettes, which *AUDIO-FILE* magazine called "The best of the bunch . . . " in a recent issue featuring storytelling for adults. In 1994, he wrote and starred in the multi-award-winning children's video, "LET'S GO TO THE FARM." Mac Parker has also recently completed work on his first novel, *Foxes and Friends,* for which he received a Vermont Council on the Arts Fellowship Grant in 1990. For further information, or to book performances, contact: Mac Parker, RD2, Box 2349, Vergennes, VT 05491, (802)877-6834.

Tom Payne started LODESTAR, a performance enhancement company, in 1983. The main focus of his work through interactive programs and business magazine articles is improving individual performance to increase organizational effectiveness. The individual's importance is also the core theme of his first book, *From the Inside Out: How to Create and Survive a Culture of Change.* Tom's next book, *A Company of One: The Power of Independence in the Workplace,* covers the benefits for the individual and organization to establish an independent culture. Tom's third book will deal with success in *FutureWork.* For information on the books or programs based on his books, contact LODESTAR at (505)296-2940 or (800)447-9254, by fax at (505)294-6942, or by mail at 1200 Lawrence Court NE, Albuquerque, NM 87123.

Rosita Perez is known as "the speaker who sings a different tune." She is the only professional speaker to be awarded all three: Council of Peers Award for Excellence and The Cavett Award from the National Speakers Association, and Speaker-of-the-Year by the National Management Association. She uses a guitar and music to share substantive messages that transform lives. A former social worker and mental health administrator, her programs re-vitalize spirits and address a different "bottom line" at conventions around the world. She is president of Creative Living Programs, Inc., and is dedicated to making a difference by speaking to hearts instead of just minds. Contact her at Creative Living Programs, 756 Fortuna Drive, Brandon, FL 33511-7963, (813)685-8267, fax (813)684-4176.

Sherry Phelan activates audiences to leverage knowledge, time, and resources with keynote speeches and seminars on "teaming and partnering." Program topics include *Profits Through Partnering* and *Creating High-Impact Results Through Team Action Planning (TAP)*. Her TAP Alliance program organizes business owners and leaders into teams twice each month as a reciprocal board of directors, for focus, problem-solving, and support to drive their businesses forward. She infuses organizations with this same spirit of entrepreneurism and commitment as she consults with company leaders and teams to improve skills in leadership, communication, teamwork and productivity. As the founder of Achievement Technology Institute, Sherry has assisted Fortune 500 companies, associations, and hundreds of growing companies since 1988. Sherry can be reached at TAP, 12 S. Raymond Avenue, Suite C, Pasadena, CA 91105, (818)577-2001.

Marianne Preger-Simon is married and the mother of two, stepmother of four, and grandmother of six. She was a founding member of Merce Cunningham's dance company and the first dance critic for *The Village Voice*. She taught music, drama, dance and literature to young people in school and community programs. She also taught psychological education at the University of Massachusetts, where she earned her doctorate before beginning a private psychotherapy practice. She leads workshops internationally, including mother/daughter workshops with her daughter, and mother/son workshops with her oldest son. Her writing has been published in various magazines and professional journals. Contact her at P.O. Box 58, Whately, MA 01093.

Andrew Proffitt was born in Bozeman, Montana, on June 12, 1981. He is 14 years old and enjoys playing all sports, as well as drawing. He grew up in Alliance, Nebraska. He also enjoys playing the drums and will be competing in Washington D.C. next summer for national competition. He is a straight "A" student.

Pastor John R. Ramsey is a highly acclaimed pastor with a motivational message that has propelled him into one of America's fastest growing ministries. Since 1991, John Ramsey has been pastor of Harvest Worship Center, a dynamic, independent, non-denominational church experiencing sustained miracle growth. His weekly television show can be seen in four states and in over 800,000 homes, and he is heard daily on the radio. In addition, John makes personal appearances at revivals, camp meetings, conventions, and seminars around the country. His writings include publication in *A 2nd Helping of Chicken Soup for the Soul*. He can be reached at John Ramsey Ministries, 3238 E. Hwy 390, Panama City, FL 32405-9305, (904)271-9647.

Naomi Rhode, RDH, CSP, CPAE, is past president of the National Speakers Association and is known for her inspirational, dynamic speaking to both health care and general audiences with whom she shares her expertise on team building, interpersonal communication, and motivation. Each year she speaks extensively at seminars, association meetings and conventions, stimulating her audiences to achieve new levels of professional and personal growth. In addition to speaking, Naomi is the author of two inspirational gift books, *The Gift of Family—A Legacy of Love* and *More Beautiful Than Diamonds—The Gift of Friendship*. Naomi Rhode can be contacted at SmartPractice, 3400 E. McDowell, Phoenix, AZ 85008-7899, (602)225-9090.

Dr. Robert Roden is the father of five children and the grandfather of five. He and his wife, Bonnie, have been married for 28 years. Bob has been an educator for 26 years. He has served as a teacher, principal, and superintendent of schools. He is currently the associate superintendent of Stark County School District. One of Bob's major volunteer activities includes speaking and facilitating in drug prevention programs for grades 7-12. Bob facilitates human relation skills workshops through Communicate Institute, Canton, Ohio, and is an adjunct professor at Walsh University. His workshops and speeches are infused with stories of personal experience, music, and a little bit of magic. Bob is currently working on three books: an illustrated version of a song he composed entitled "I Am Special"; a book on self-esteem for young people called "You Are Loved"; and another on parenting called "Sand in the Garage." He can be reached at 1107 Glendale SW, North Canton, OH 44720, (216)494-2648.

Peggy L. Rolfsmeyer is a teacher, educational consultant, and licensed counselor. In her career she has taught elementary school, worked with adolescent girls living in a group home, given workshops on self-esteem and communication skills, and supervised student teachers for Eastern Michigan University. She has also supervised counseling interns for the University of Pittsburgh in Pennsylvania. As an independent contractor for Performance Learning Systems, Inc., she is currently teaching graduate education courses in Pennsylvania. She has also taught these courses in Michigan and Kansas through Marygrove College and Ft. Hays State University respectively. Peggy can be contacted at 31 Tankard Lane, Washington Crossing, PA 18977.

Dan Rosandich promotes himself with a brochure entitled "Cartoonist for Hire." Interested parties are invited to phone or fax him at (906)482-6234 supplying a scenario or description of the idea or cartoon they'd like to have illustrated. In turn, Dan will pencil in roughs and fax them to you for approval or for any changes before a final inking is given to the work. The artist guarantees next day delivery by Fedex or UPS overnight. His work appears nationally in such magazines as *First for Women, Boy's Life,* and *National Enquirer.* Rosandich has been professionally involved in all aspects of cartooning since 1977 when he sold his first cartoon to *Mechanix Illustrated* magazine, which has since folded. CALL HIM!

Jane Sanders is a professional speaker and trainer with nearly 20 years of sales and marketing experience. She has presented to over 300 small businesses and Fortune 500 audiences. Jane's topics include: "Success From The Inside Out"—a powerful and customized motivational program on personal and professional growth; "Men & Women: Communicating Effectively at Work"—a well-researched review of gender differences, how they affect communication, and what to do about them; and sales presentation skills. Jane is known for her warm, down-to-earth style and impassioned, captivating presentations. She uses powerful personal stories, quotes, statistics, and exercises to teach and inspire her audiences. Contact her at Empowerment Enterprises, 4601 Alla Road, Suite 4, Marina del Rey, CA 90292, (310)306-4546, fax (310)827-0776.

John Schmitt is a psychology teacher at McDowell High School in Erie, Pennsylvania. Since 1982 he has also worked as an educational consultant with teachers across the country to improve their effectiveness in the classroom. In this capacity he has trained over 2000 educators in the nine graduate education courses developed by Performance Learning Systems (PLS). Most recently he served as an associate designer for the newest PLS course: Teaching the Skills of the 21st Century. For information on staff development workshops or graduate education seminars, contact John at (814)838-2559.

Dexter Schraer is a teacher and administrator for the Columbia Public Schools in Columbia, Missouri. He loves speaking in public, frozen M&Ms, cooking, reading, and landscaping. He believes in magic, the dreams of children, and the power of print. He has been awarded academic degrees from Westminster College, the University of Iowa, and Saint Louis University. He is the founder of Just Say Yes, a highlight-the-positive consulting firm. He lives with his family at 830 Court Street, Fulton, MO 65251. He can be reached by telephone at (314)642-4075.

Julianna Simon is a family counselor and a writer. Her work is devoted to the interface between psychology, spirituality, and community. She leads workshops nationwide, including father-daughter workshops with her father, Dr. Sidney Simon; mother-daughter workshops with her mother, Dr. Marianne Simon; and "sibling revelry" workshops with her brother, John. She is currently writing a book with her father, *Fathers and Daughters: Finding the Harmonies, Healing the Wounds;* and a second book, *Ninety-Five Dinner Table Conversations to Nourish Family Values.* For further information about her work, write RD2, Box 2349, Vergennes, VT 05491, or contact Simon Workshops, 45 Old Mountain Road, Hadley, MA 01035.

Dr. Sidney B. Simon is an internationally known pioneer in Psychological Education. He has recently retired from teaching after being on the firing line for 40 years. For the past 20 years he has taught at the University of Massachusetts in Amherst, and he will continue to conduct workshops all over the United States, Canada, Mexico, and Europe. He is one of the authors of the four classic books in Values Clarification: *Values and Teaching; Values Clarification: A Handbook of Practical Strategies; Clarifying Values Through Subject Matter;* and *Meeting Yourself Halfway.* Combined, they have sold close to two million copies. Sid is a husband and a father of five children, several of whom have become counselors and teachers, about which he feels justifiably proud. His latest book, *Forgiveness: How to Make Peace with Your Past and Get on with Your Future,* was co-authored with his wife, Suzanne. Contact him at 1757 Venus Drive, Sanibel, FL 33957, (413)584-4382.

Joanna Slan is a motivational speaker who focuses on helping people adjust their attitudes by adding more joy and enthusiasm to their lives. She has presented in four countries and all across the United States. Her programs include *Are We Having Fun Yet?*, *I'm Too Blessed to Be Depressed*, and *Lifebalance Strategies*. Joanna is the author of two books: *I'm Too Blessed to Be Depressed: Stories to Uplift and Inspire* and *If Mama Ain't Happy, Ain't Nobody Happy: How Women Can Break the Rules to Create Happier Lives*. For more information about Joanna's books or speaking services, call 1-800-356-2220 or fax (314)530-7970. In St. Louis, Missouri, drop on by! But call (314)530-7667 first so she can scoop the papers off the chairs.

Joshua "Josh" Smothers is 14 years old and lives in Cedar Rapids, Iowa, with his parents, J.J. and Cindy, and his three siblings, Tyler, 11, Erica, 7, and Samantha, 4. He was born May 29, 1981, in Cedar Rapids, Iowa, and, amazingly, three years later Tyler was born on May 29, 1984! Maybe this is one of the reasons why Josh and Tyler have a special bond. He loves to play basketball and recently was in Frankfort, Kentucky, for a 14-and-under AAU National Basketball Tournament. Josh is 6'1" and weighs 160 pounds. He also likes to play baseball and was in a 13-and-under AAU National Baseball Tournament. He enjoys football and track. The fun thing about playing sports for Josh is that Tyler is always there to cheer him on. Tyler is without a doubt Josh's number one fan! Josh enjoys school and maintained a 3.85 grade point average during his middle school career. You can contact him at (319)396-0636.

Dr. Cecelia J. Soares is a dynamic and entertaining professional speaker. She has a unique triple background: veterinary medicine, marriage and family therapy, and education. She presents to the business community as well as to general audiences. Cecelia speaks on a number of topics, many of which are motivational and inspirational. In these talks, she uses powerful stories which draw from real life experiences. She is particularly interested in the relationships between people and their animals and has done research on the role of dogs in families. Cecelia has been married for 27 years and has two grown children, and she has survived two life-threatening illnesses. She can be contacted at ViewPoint Consultation & Seminars, 2757 West Newell Ave., Walnut Creek CA 94595, (510)932-0607.

Leslie Krauz Stambaugh has spent over 20 years consulting with organizations on management issues. She has helped hundreds of companies provide more fulfilling (and less frustrating) work climates *while* increasing their bottom lines! She focuses on customer-centered strategies—using market sensitivity, effective management practices, and streamlined work processes—to achieve organizational goals. Her success as a consultant and speaker begins and ends with careful listening and clear communication—understanding not only what is said, but also what is meant. And the changes she triggers: Build on people's strengths—and on their diversity. Get people to give their best for a common goal. And result in outcomes where everybody—management, employees, *and* customers—win. To contact Leslie Stambaugh call RLS Associates at (313)769-6300.

Jane Stroschin is an author and illustrator of nine books. She has spoken at Young Author Celebrations all over America. At 150 schools per year, her fun-filled presentations inspire students to use their talents. In Jane's children's book, *A Unicorn Named Beulah Mae*, she writes: " . . . you have special gifts too, enjoy who you are, you-niquely you!" The core of her books and workshops is self-esteem. "Discover your gifts, your talents, and use them ABUNDANTLY." Jane's newest book, *Fingertip Friends*, is designed as letters between a U.S. soldier in Vietnam and his mother. "I wrote this book for the soldiers who served there and for their families who waited and prayed back home." Contact her at Henry Quill Press, 7340 Lake Drive, Fremont, MI 49412, (616)924-3026.

Ann Tait is 14 years old and a freshman in high school. She lives in the small town of Alliance, Nebraska, with her parents, Don and Sandy, one sister, Christi, and, of course, her brother, Jimmy. She plays piano, swims, and is very involved in church activities, and she loves to write. Just this past year she began to send some of her writing out. She won a local newspaper essay contest, got an award of recognition from a nationwide contest, and also placed in a speech contest. If you would like to contact her, the address is 1424 Boise, Alliance, NE 69301, (308)762-6781.

Dottie Walters began her tiny advertising business on foot, pushing her two babies before her on a rickety stroller built for one child. She tied a pillow on the back of the stroller with clothesline, put cardboard in her shoes, and never gave up. She was determined that they would not lose their home. She had no college education, so she read every book she could find about people of achievement at the public library. She hears the voices in the books and still reads six or seven biographies a week. Dottie built her business into all of Southern California, with four offices and 285 employees. Her speaking career has taken her all over the world. She is the author of many books and audio albums. She publishes the leading magazine in the world of professional paid speaking, *Sharing Ideas,* and is the president of Walters International Speakers Bureau. She is a well known international speaker and a professional consultant. Contact her at P.O. Box 1120, Glendora, CA 91740, phone (818)335-8069, fax (818)335-6127.

Mildred H. Walton came into the world as an identical twin in 1904. In 1930 she married Aubrey G. Walton, a Methodist preacher. In the early years of her marriage she was often introduced to women who told her, "I could never marry a preacher." Her standard response became, "Neither could I. I married the man I loved, and his profession came with him." Since she wrote "Grandmother's Christmas" in 1968, Mildred has presented it at least 200 times—without notes—to groups throughout Arkansas and Louisiana. By her own admission, "Aubrey's 12 years as resident Bishop in Louisiana may have been responsible for many of my invitations!" She currently resides at 510 Brookside Dr. #73, Little Rock, AR 72205.

Terry Wooten as a poet-bard takes his oral poetry and workshop program to thousands each year. He is a living anthology of classic literature, ancient and contemporary poetry, children's selections and his own work rich in humor and lore, presented in an entertaining and educational package. He has published five books and has been included in numerous publications. Terry is also the builder and host-poet of the Stone Circle, a triple ring of 88 large boulders capturing the atmosphere of ancient cultures that gathered in family and community groups to exchange stories of everyday life and lore. Around a flickering campfire listeners perch on boulders as words wash over them like the stars. For further information call (616)264-9467, or write to 12754 Stone Circle Dr., Kewadin, MI 49648.

Rhoda D. Zagorsky is a professional speaker, healer, and facilitator. She enables people to live better through meditation, hands on healing, and reflexology. Her work since 1982 is best expressed as a triangle representing body, mind and emotions. Rhoda has produced two meditation tapes, "Claim Your Birthright" and "Personal Peace Through Forgiveness." She is a member of the National Speakers Association and is co-founder of "The Healing Touch" program (classes, lectures and services). Contact her at 397 Winthrop St., Medford, MA 02155, (617)395-5680.

Chick Moorman is the director of the Institute For Personal Power, a consulting firm dedicated to providing high-quality professional development activities for educators and parents.

He is a former classroom teacher with over 25 years of experience in the field of education. His mission is to help people experience a greater sense of personal power in their lives so they can, in turn, empower others.

Chick conducts full-day workshops and seminars for school districts and parent groups. He also delivers keynote addresses for local, state, and national conferences.

He is available for the following topic areas:

FOR PARENTS
- Raising Your Child's Self-Esteem
- Parent Talk: What It Really Means
- Empowered Parenting
- Building Family Solidarity
- Developing Positive Attitudes in Children

FOR EDUCATORS
- Teaching Respect and Responsibility
- Improving Student Self-Esteem
- Stamping Out Learned Helplessness
- Teacher Talk: What It Really Means
- Cooperative Learning
- Teaching Proud
- Dealing with Reluctant Learners

If you'd like more information about these programs or would like to discuss a possible training or speaking date, please contact the Institute For Personal Power, P.O. Box 5985, Saginaw, MI 48603 or call (517)791-3533.

Chick Moorman